SOUL
Dance

Soul Dance

Karen Rose Kobylka

Published by Karen Rose Kobylka, 2024.

SOUL DANCE

First edition. March 3, 2024.

ISBN: 978-1738329304

Written by Karen Rose Kobylka.

Table of Contents

To Sir, with Love

Disclaimer:

This is a memoir. The author wishes to make it clear that this book is not intended to harm, harass, or defame any individual, group, or community. The views expressed herein are solely those of the author and do not reflect the opinions or beliefs of any particular spiritual or religious community. The author has no ill will toward any spiritual or religious group and intends this work as a form of self-expression.

This book is not meant to be a commentary on any specific religious or spiritual practices, and any interpretations or assumptions made by readers are their own. The author disclaims any liability for potential misunderstandings, misinterpretations, or perceived harm resulting from the content of this book.

"We need to save ourselves, and be our own fairy Godmother, buy our own glass slippers and strut our stuff. Be happy for who we truly are and love ourselves."

-Karen Rose Kobylka-

Acknowledgments

To everyone who contributed to the realization of *Soul Dance*, whether through feedback, encouragement, or simply by being a part of this creative journey, thank you for being a vital and cherished part of this meaningful endeavor.

I would like to express my deepest gratitude to Amy and Jenny, my dedicated editors, whose unwavering support and invaluable insight played an instrumental role in bringing *Soul Dance* to life. Your commitment to refining and enhancing my work has been truly exceptional, and I am immensely thankful for your expertise and guidance.

A heartfelt thank-you also extends to my new community, a source of inspiration and support. I am grateful for the warmth and acceptance I've found among you, and your encouragement has fueled my creative journey.

A special appreciation goes to my sister, who showed up at two in the morning, a beacon of support and love, attempting to save me. Your presence in my life is a constant reminder of the strength that comes from family bonds. Thank you for being my anchor in challenging times.

With sincere appreciation,
Karen Rose Kobylka

Introduction

TBH (to be honest)

Have you ever felt the need to address the challenges you've faced? Well, this book began as a way for me to process and overcome the difficulties I experienced within the spiritual community. Initially driven by a desire for vindication, the act of putting my thoughts onto paper became a therapeutic journey. Over the years, I discovered that writing this book not only facilitated my own soul's evolution but also presented an opportunity to help others understand their own stories on a profound level. My new goal is to offer insight and share my personal journey, in the hope that it may resonate with others and aid them in understanding their own soul stories.

What defined me in the past was my role as a business owner and a hairstylist for over 38 years. I successfully owned and operated a thriving beauty business. I generated yearly revenues exceeding $350,000.00. I managed a network of 16 beauty salons across the province of Alberta. While I found success in both business and hairstyling, I failed to recognize that my career was gradually taking a toll on my well-being, as well as on my personal life. I felt it was essential to share my income during my successful career. It's crucial for people to understand that mental illness can affect individuals from all walks of life. Despite my financial success, I found myself grappling with mental health challenges. It serves as a stark reminder that mental health issues can impact anyone, regardless of their background or financial status.

Unbeknownst to me, I began to delve into gambling, unaware of the undiagnosed mental illness that was silently afflicting me. I found myself squandering what should have been my retirement savings on slot machines. Deep within, I sensed a pervasive discontentment, yet I struggled to identify its source. Despite seemingly possessing everything, including a common-law marriage and financial prosperity, a profound sense of discontent continued to persist.

In an attempt to seek happiness, I made what I believed was the right decision – leaving my common-law husband and embarking on a new chapter of my life. Little did I know, an undiagnosed demon lurked within me, in the form of bipolar disorder, which would eventually escalate into episodes of mania and psychosis.

After my mother crossed over into the spiritual realm, spirit, or ghosts (what some people call them), showed me that I was a born spiritual medium. I started to hear, see and feel spirit all around me. So, I turned to a church of spirituality, where they believe we cross over to spirit when we die, and that mediums can communicate with the deceased. Some spiritual people believe in the soul and how people can be in touch with their soul and help it grow in order to be a better person. I dove deep into this concept, the society, and their philosophy. It became a way of life for me.

I believed in spirituality so much I packed my bags and took my soul on a journey. I relocated to British Columbia, specifically Vancouver Island, where my mentor, a respected figure in mediumship, and a reverend, was based. He played a significant role in the spiritual community on the Island and was widely recognized as a renowned medium.

My goal with this new move, was to expand my booming hair salon business to British Columbia and franchise it. I was on fire! My plans were to conquer the world. I had so much energy, enthusiasm, and pride for what I was doing. There was no doubt in my mind that I would succeed. I had a spice for life when I first arrived on the Island of Hope. I called it "the Island of Hope". Hope for a fresh start and a soul-driven purposeful life. I would take courses and workshops on mediumship, spirituality, the soul, and the Law of Attraction. It was my favourite thing to do. Growing myself on a spiritual level started to fuel my soul.

I wish I could share with you that I am back on track financially, spiritually, and mentally. The real truth of the matter is that we are never finished growing. I rent a single room from a young lady for a modest fee for five years. It has a bed, side table and a dresser. In the corner you will find my bookshelf where I have accumulated my tarot card collection, the only thing that I have of worth. I have no savings at all; I live on provincial disability because of my bipolar disorder. This situation exists because I had no safety net when mental illness crept in. When I reached out for help-everyone ran. That was the circumstance that left me with my current reality. My landlady is selling her condo and I need to move out. On to a new adventure. I have learned to accept change.

I'll be frank—living with bipolar disorder and embracing my role as a medium and empath is a tough journey. My emotions are like a roller coaster. I suffer from depression and take no medication for it because I hate taking medication. I do, however, take a monthly injection called Abilify for my bipolar disorder. This medication helps me from turning manic, and psychotic. I have had both, as you will read about later in my story. The medication keeps me balanced and able to live a full life that is happy and healthy. I go regularly to my psychiatrist who keeps me in check, making sure I remain balanced. I consider myself blessed to have a great doctor of psychiatry to help me on this rather new journey in my life.

Considering that I lost everything that I have ever had in my life-—friends, money, and belongings due to betrayal or mayhem, I am doing rather well these days. I feel blessed in my life. When I was running my beauty empire, I never felt blessed. I have $18 in the bank until my next disability cheque. I go to the food bank for groceries to help me survive and I still feel blessed. When you come close to Heaven's Gate, due to a suicide attempt, and everything you have ever loved has been taken away from you, and you are given a second chance to do it all over again by the Great Spirit or who some call God, you start to appreciate the little things in life.

I am currently working on furthering my education by taking life, spiritual, and soul coaching courses to help others who need some spiritual insight into their life. This is my new passion. It is proving to be rather challenging due to lack of finances, but I am doing it little by little, step by step. Some may say "What does she have to offer anyone while living on disability with a mental disorder?" I can tell you that through this disaster which I encountered with the spiritual church, I have found the real me, deep inside the rubble from the breakdown that I had. I have overcome this destruction. I have found the real meaning of life, and although it is not complete, I find myself happy in this life. I am happier than I have ever been despite the challenges that I face.

After my mental illness and the spiritual church incident, I found myself with no friends and very few family members believing in me. With the exception of two friends from my old life that I have had to rekindle, I had to build my network of friends from scratch. This is proving to be the most difficult of all my challenges. This island that I once called an "Island of Hope" has lost its allure. I have a few friends who help me survive the day-to-day stresses of being poor. They help me by giving me love. We are all searching for Love. I do have that, from people who only a few years ago were perfect strangers and are now the reason that I carry on.

My soul continues to shine bright these days despite the traumas I have endured. This book is about my soul, and the island that I once called Hope is now called Faith. I have faith that things will turn out better than I could ever "hope" for.

Glossary of Terminology

Aura
An aura is a field of energy, radiating colors which surround the entire body.

Bipolar Disorder
Bipolar Disorder is characterized by extremities of high and low mood. It is a mental condition marked by alternating periods of elation and deep depression. Bipolar involves experiencing emotions on a grand scale.

Clair Senses
Clair- means 'clear' in French. It is a different way of sensing and perceiving information from the different senses.

1. Clairvoyant (clear seeing) receives impressions in the mind by way of mental images. I sometimes see visions of spirits as if they were right in front of me. I sometimes see auras.

2. Claircognizance (clear knowing) - an ability to know things about the future. You just know it.

3. Clairaudient (clear hearing) - when you can hear sounds, words, or noise from Spirit.

4. Clairsentient (clear physical feeling) - a physical sensation in your body.

5. Clairtangency (clear touching) - distinguishing facts about an event or person by contact with the object or person. It is also commonly known as psychometry.

6. Clairalience (clear smelling) - smelling odors from the spirit world to give you messages, rather than the odors which are perceived by the nose.

7. Clairgustance (clear tasting) - receiving psychic information through sense of taste; the taste comes directly from Spirit and not from oneself.

Coping mechanisms

Something a person does to deal with a difficult situation; certain habits that act as outlets for stress.

Crystal Personality

A rare life color that radiates around the body. It is clear and can change its color to reflect who they are hanging out with at the time. They can take on the life color of other people surrounding the crystal personality. A Crystal's gift is to help heal people and clear any blockages that they might have.

Destination Addiction

Destination addiction is the idea that happiness is somewhere else.

Domino Effect

A situation in which something happens, causing other similar events to happen. If it involves good emotions, then good will come. If it involves negative emotion, then more negative emotions will follow. It is emotional energy running swiftly. It is the Law of Attraction.

Emotional Freedom Technique-(EFT/Tapping)

Tapping is a technique which connects the body to the mind, much like acupuncture. Acupuncture is a Chinese practice of inserting fine needles through the skin at specific points, especially to cure disease or relieve pain. Tapping is doing this with the fingertips of your hands. Tapping on the energy system pathways, known as meridians, shifts the energies. When verbally or mentally addressing the root cause of the emotional distress, the areas of blocked energy are then able to release. Simply focus on the negative emotion you have and then tap on the meridians.

Empath

Empaths are highly sensitive. They absorb the feelings and emotions of others. Empaths tune into subtle energies surrounding each person's body. They can feel what people don't say. Their ability to absorb the energy around them may make it difficult for them to watch certain kinds of programs.

Emotional Blockages

Unfelt or suppressed emotions like anger, resentment, and guilt: dense emotions that block energy/auric fields. If we do not remove emotional blocks which are stored in our auric field energy, we can never truly feel at peace. Blockages can even be passed down from your parents.

Emotions and The Law of Attraction

Your emotions are a signposts from your soul as to whether you are on the right track in life. The Law of Attraction is the most powerful law in the universe. You are creating your reality every moment of every day. You are creating your future with every single thought, either consciously or subconsciously. You cannot take a break from it and decide not to create because creation never stops. Understanding your emotions is very important. If you fail to understand your emotions, it can turn your life upside down.

Emotional Ladder

The Emotional Ladder is derived from the Abraham Hicks Emotional Guidance Scale, which maps the range of emotions experienced in life. On this scale, "One" represents the highest vibrational emotions, while "Twelve" signifies the lowest. This tool serves as a means to enhance your self-awareness regarding your current emotional state. By gaining a better understanding of your emotions, you can strive to elevate your vibration to its highest potential. Neglecting negative emotions for extended periods can adversely impact your physical well-being, potentially leading to ailments, disorders, and diseases. This underscores the significance of maintaining emotional awareness. Utilizing the Emotional Ladder can facilitate a deeper connection with your emotional landscape.

Karma

Karma is energy reflected back at you. This is part of everyday vibration and alignment. If you do wrong, wrong will come back to you. You will experience the destiny that you earn through your actions and behavior. It is the Law of Attraction—what you give out comes back to you.

Mania

Mania can be mild, moderate, or severe. At times, all you see is a fun, optimistic, and upbeat person, the life of the party; other times, you may notice irregular behaviors. A person who has developed mania may become more talkative, to the point where others cannot get a word in. You have tons of energy and do not want to stop.

Medium

A medium is a person who can connect with a spirit that has passed on. Mediums know the difference between their thoughts and the ones coming from the spirit.

Mediumship Mixed with Mental Illness

One should fully understand who they are and what their demons are, in order to be a well-rounded medium. One must know one's soul and the layers it has. As a medium, one needs to understand the difference between a healthy brain and an unhealthy brain. One works with understanding one's thoughts. You are trained to clear your mind. When the mind is clear from thoughts, one can hear Spirit's messages.

When a medium is in trauma and utter despair and having a nervous breakdown, they are in a spiritual emergency. There is a fine line between a healthy brain and an unhealthy one. With mediumship, you are working with your conscious and subconscious mind. When your mind is ill, mediumship can become disastrous.

Psychosis

Psychosis disrupts the typical functioning of the mind, causing an individual to disconnect from reality. Symptoms may include hallucinations, delusions, and other psychotic manifestations. Those who experience psychosis may grapple with distorted thoughts and perceptions, often manifested through vivid hallucinations and irrational beliefs. This altered state of mind can lead individuals to experience events that are not grounded in reality and adopt beliefs that are detached from the actual circumstances.

Soul

Each person has a soul which is unique to them. It is your highest power, your guiding force that is connected to your energy body, which encompasses your physical body. It has all the answers you seek, connecting to the Great Spirit, God or Source Energy. Many people believe that your soul continues to exist after your body is dead. The soul is the highest level that you can reach for. It is connected to your intuition. The soul is all about love. It is the aspect of who and what you are. If you take a moment to listen to its whispers, it brings you closer to the Great Spirit and the universe. The soul is eternally yours.

Ego

The ego is about the self. Ego is essentially one's perception of their own value, encompassing both positive and negative aspects.

Spirit

Spirit, derived from the Latin word meaning 'breath,' represents the energy or essence within a person. It permeates the world around us, serving as a guiding force, leading us back to our origin. The goal of spirit is to align with our pure soul's purpose, illuminating our path towards spiritual enlightenment.

SPIRITUAL HEALING

Spiritual healing is a process which encompasses the transfer of energy, connecting spiritual energy to the recipient's mind, body, and spirit. It is a tangible and achievable phenomenon. The healing unfolds as Spirit orchestrates the when and how of the restoration process.

The different types of spiritual healing are as follows:

- Magnetic Healing is the transference of energy from one person to another.
- Absent Healing: Spirit healing without contact.
- Distant Healing: giving healing to a person from a distance.
- Near to the Body Healing: contact healing with the hands removed a few centimeters away.
- Trance Healing: usually takes the same pattern as contact healing, but in this form, the healer allows himself to be enveloped by Spirit.

Soul Journey/Soul Story

A soul journey is taken in order to find a deeper meaning of self. It can be tumultuous. Through the process of life, there are ups and downs. These ups and downs come with life lessons. If you choose to see them this way, you can uncover these spiritual lessons and learn to live life to the fullest.

Social Anxiety

Social anxiety is the fear of social situations that involve interaction with other people. It is the fear of being negatively judged and evaluated by other people.

Telepathy

Telepathy is communication between two people using their minds, without words.

Twin Flame

"Twin flames" refers to two souls who connect on a deep soul level. A twin flame can come into your life to teach you valuable life lessons. However, it is said that twin flames cannot be together unless they have learned their life lessons and are vibrationally a match.

The Law of Attraction

The Law of Attraction is attracting positive and negative situations into your life through thoughts and actions.

Trance

An altered state of awareness, much like being hypnotized, a half-conscious state.

Vibration

Everything in the universe has a frequency: thoughts, feelings, and emotions.

Chapter One- Once Upon a Time

O nce upon a time, in the heart of August 1968, on a sultry night aglow with the brilliance of a full moon, the Misericordia Hospital in Alberta, Canada became the backdrop for a pivotal moment: Lena's labor, destined to bring forth a Crystal Child into the world. Lena was a medium who had bipolar disorder. Lena was unaware of her abilities and her disorder. This made Lena's journey through life very challenging. When Lena gave birth to her first and only child, she named the baby Karen. The meaning of the name Karen is "pure", and that is why Lena named her newborn baby Karen. That baby was me and this is my soul story. Everyone on earth has a soul story, and a soul purpose as to why we are brought into this world. It took me my entire life to find out who I was and why I was here on earth. So, when it came time to write my memoir I wanted to start with the very beginning when the universe was conspiring to create me. As it happened through writing my memoir, I realized why I was born. And how I, Karen, could fulfil my purpose here on earth.

My purpose was never clear to me until while writing this book I had memories of the old crone who came to visit me. It was an epic moment, one that I would never forget. When I was just a young girl, an old crone dressed in a tattered gray cape approached me and told me that I was an empath and a Crystal Child. She explained that I was a child who could help change the world if I used my gift of communicating with the dead. This bewildered me as I found the crone to be cryptic and mystifying. Nonetheless, she held my attention with her words. She told me that I was unique, and that I was brought onto this earth to help shed light to others, to help change the world and spread love. I was also told that I would one day write a book that would help people. When I asked her what the book would be about—the crone disappeared. That moment changed my life and helped me to believe in something greater than myself.

Looking back, I can understand now that the old crone was there as my spirit guide to help me understand my gifts. I remember having vivid dreams and nightmares as a young child. The dreams I had would always come true. This was frightening to me. I remember dreaming of a person dying. Within the next few days, they would be dead. During this time, I remember praying to God to help me because these dramatic dreams frightened me. I was afraid of these ghosts. I did not understand my gift back then.

Ever since I can remember, I felt awkward and different from others. As long as I can remember, I have had the ability to see ghosts (or spirits as I call them now). They frightened me, and I hated the thought of bedtime as a result. Each night the ghosts would surround me before I slept. As I became older, the ghosts would send me messages in my dreams. I remember when I saw one of my first ghosts. I was sick with the stomach flu, and I was asleep in bed. Suddenly, I had an inspiration to open my eyes. I saw a little boy in a sixteenth century, beautifully crafted costume, standing in front of my bed. The little boy spirit was so vivid that he looked real. He told me his name was Zachary. He scared the wits out of me, and I screamed as loud as my little voice could. Then he disappeared. Later that week, a boy named Zachary enrolled in my class at school. That is the way my life has been, a lot of serendipity moments.

Reflecting back on my life, as long as I can remember I could always see spirit and feel people's emotions. I thought this was normal. It was as if I could feel their pain, read their thoughts, and feel what they are feeling. This caused me to be anxious, frazzled, and nervous around people throughout my entire life because I did not understand what was happening to me. It did not help that I could tell whether they were a good or bad person. I would get images from spirit that would give me predictions of events that were to happen in the days, weeks, and months to come and they would always come true. It wasn't until my 54 years of living on this earth that I started to fully realize that I am an *empath*, and I was actually a *born* spiritual medium with *bipolar disorder*. This was a formula for disaster, because I never knew who I was on a soul level. I did not understand who I was and why I did the things that I did. In one situation I could be outgoing and extravagant in my reactions and the next I would be shy and standoffish. That is bipolar. What I understand now is that I could always read people psychically despite my mental illness.

Until a lifetime of soul searching, studying spirituality as well as the Law of Attraction, I did not realize that this law could affect my life so extensively. People's emotions are contagious and if you are not centered in who you are, you can easily become infected by the other person's vibration. If someone around me was sad or in despair, I would soon pick up these emotions and absorb them unknowingly, causing my vibration to plummet to the ground and my alignment to go down the tube. This caused me to be depressed and unsure of who I was.

In my late forties the spiritual church took me under their wing and led me to the Great Spirit. I started to dive deeply into soul growth, trying to fully understand who I was. I came up with no answers. It wasn't until I completely snapped and lost all mental faculties and was charged with criminal harassment that I began to realize that my life was much more than just past events, that every event in our lives shapes us to who we are today. Everything that happens from the start of your life lies inside the mind. Thoughts and actions carry vibration. What were people's emotions that surrounded the mother? How were you cared for? These are all the vibrations which lie inside your subconscious mind and shape you as you are today.

It is all remembered in our soul. A newborn is aware of the emotions which surround it. They carry these emotions with them throughout life. The memories that we have at our birth is the start of your soul story. It is the key to your soul purpose and to find out who you really are on a soul level. These birth memories also carry a vibration, positive or negative. This vibration will start the domino effect in your life. In other words, if you have good emotions surrounding your birth, good continues. If you have a negative situation at birth, negative feelings will continue. Unless you are well aware of these emotions, the same emotions will continue. That is the Law of Attraction.

What I have come to notice while writing *Soul Dance* is that all my emotions stem from my birth. When I was born, my parents had just married. My conception was a surprise to them. Years before I was born, my father had been happily married with four young toddlers. His wife died at the early age of 29. It left him a widower with four young children to raise. My father's mother, Mary, took over the care of the children during the week while my father was at work. They managed this way for several years. This took its toll on the family. The youngest child was named Donna. She was just a baby when her mother Lorna died. After that, Donna went to stay with her father's sister Gladys. Gladys and Donna soon developed a bond. Everyone was in mourning and the vibration was heavy.

The entire family was grieving, not just my father and his children, but his surrounding family. It was then that my father's illness would start to manifest slowly and unknowingly. He would develop severe heart ailments later in life. Nonetheless, these were already in motion at the young age of 32 by way of vibration. All of this was because he didn't release the negative emotions caused by his wife dying. These negative emotions became emotional blockages.

A few years later, my mother came into the picture. She was brought into a family which was still vibrating at a lower frequency due to grief. My mother was vibrating at the same frequency as my father. She too had emotional blockages from her mother and father dying when she was 13 years old. Thus my mother and father were a vibrational match for each other. When my mother Lena and father Edward met, they were both in grieving, and so were the children. There is no set timetable for grief. All people grieve differently. My father's grief ran deep. He remained strong and was determined to start a new life when he met my mother. However, as a baby, I felt the vibration of grieving the loss of his wife. It sounds crazy, but I understood this concept as I grew up and I knew how difficult it would have been on him and the family. He was an amazing man, and I loved him dearly.

My father and mother dated for awhile and my mother came to be close to his children. My father asked my mother to marry him shortly after they became pregnant with me. After my mother and my father married, it was a shock to the family who was still grieving his former wife, Lorna. As a result, my mother wore a yellow wedding dress to signify the old-fashioned stigma even though it was my mother's first marriage. She missed the chance to wear a white wedding dress. This saddened me when I found out. My mother took on the role of mother, caregiver, homemaker, and wife to Edward and his four children. She was only 22 years old.

When my mother first moved into the house that Lorna and Edward had lived in with their young children, it proved to be difficult as she was trying to fit into a life that was not her own. Edward's family did their best to welcome her into the family, but the dynamics proved to be complicated. I feel that this was because of the vibration that had occurred due to Lorna's death. My mother did her best to fit in but never quite felt like she belonged. This was the energy and vibration carried forward to me as a young baby, toddler, adolescent, and finally adult. Today I still struggle with trying to fit in, because of vibrational energy and emotions I carry as a result of all this.

Once my mother had given birth to me and settled in, Donna, the youngest child, came back to live in the household from her aunt's place when she was four years old. Gladys (my dad's sister) was emotional, of course, because she was now mourning the loss of Donna's presence. This vibration carried my mother further into not fitting in with the family, and my Baba (grandmother Mary, my father's mother) did not give Lena the chance to fit in properly. Mary too was mourning the loss of her daughter-in-law Lorna. Mary was accustomed to looking after the children, and now someone else would be doing that job. These emotions proved to be a strain on my mother's and Mary's relationship. All these vibrations affected me as a young child. During this time, my father was still grieving his wife Lorna's death. He was worried about his youngest child Donna, as she was ill with a hole in her heart. Worrying can drain your energy and instill fear. It can distract you, muddy up your decision-making process and prolong suffering.

A year later, Donna died at 6 years of age. I sensed an aura of sadness enveloping the family. As an adult, I can now comprehend why my father was emotionally reserved with me during this period. I felt this vibration as a baby, and it has carried on with me to this day. I can now understand this as an emotional blockage. Donna's death sent shockwaves through our family. Back then, no one went to counseling, and the grief was brushed under the carpet. As everyone was grieving this loss, my oldest sister remembers being told not to cry by our Baba Mary. I was too young to understand what had happened during this time, but I do have memories of Donna and how close we were as children.

After Donna's death, I remember the feelings of loneliness. My other half-siblings were older and did not play with me. I was much too young for them. I grew up like an only child. Although I have fond memories of our family growing up, I was lonely. I was not raised to believe that this family was my half family. We were raised as a complete family unit. The age gap between myself and my half-siblings was the main reason we didn't grow up together. I spent a lot of time by myself. I had nobody to play with at home. Thus, I developed a strong sense of social independence where I'd create stories in my head. Little did I know Spirit was helping me—I was, after all, a born medium. If you have a large enough gap between yourself and your siblings, you're probably more like an only child.

Donna's death had repercussions for all of us. However, my father did his best to carry on. He did rather well, considering the agony he was going through. I do remember looking at old family pictures and films to find out that when Edward's first wife Lorna was still alive, my father was very engaged with his family. There were lots of photos, memories, and films of his wife Lorna and the family. After Lorna and Donna died, and Lena and Edward had me, Edward was still grieving. Therefore, there were no videos and not many pictures of me. The family photo albums and videos reflected this very strongly. This is not to imply anything negative about my father. I recognize that he was grieving, and that his grief was too much for him to handle. I understand that, and honor him with this book. I also saw that when I was about ten years old, the photos and films started again, and my father was more engaged in my life. It signified to me that he was then healing from the loss that he had experienced.

The simple fact of the matter is that the emotions were sad in the household after my sister Donna died, and nothing was the same after that. I felt these emotions even as a baby. During this time, while my father was healing, my mother took on the burden of running the household while at the same time suffering from rheumatoid arthritis and undiagnosed bipolar disorder. My mother's arthritis was crippling. She did not, however, let it stop her from running the household.

My mother struggled in her life from a mental illness she knew nothing about. She was not aware of her bipolar disorder. My mother's mood swings became more evident as time went by and my two older sisters had a difficult time with this while they were growing up. It put a strain on our household. The vibration was heavy which I picked up on as a young child. My mother was a farm girl who had moved to the city to go to secretarial school. She then met my father. She was a very hard worker and was not afraid of the challenge of taking on four children and then me. She took on the role of mother and wife very well while having a mental illness she knew nothing about.

When I was a little girl, I was empathetic and intuitive, so my mother's and father's vibrations and emotions played on my vibration to such an extent that I felt my mother was consumed with worry and grief. This vibration affected the entire family's dynamics. As a young child, I would avoid burdening my mother with my troubles. I would keep all my problems to myself. I would not even tell my siblings about my troubles. When I was growing up, I felt everyone's emotions.

When my father Edward was first a widower, my oldest sister was in grade one. Her teacher, Mrs. Orr, was made aware of her mother's death. Mrs. Orr told my oldest sister that she would keep her and take her home to adopt her. When Mrs. Orr finally found out that she was not to take my sister home and keep her, she was sad. Later she took this sadness out on me when I went to her school. Mrs. Orr bullied me, and this fueled the vibration for my classmates that this behavior was acceptable. I wasn't in my power of alignment because of the negative vibrations around me. Thus, I was not able to defend myself.

I did not tell my family that Mrs. Orr treated me the way she did. I remember that when I was in class, she would stand over me as I tried to complete the assignments. This caused me stress and trauma to such a degree that I would shut down and cry. It also caused me to have difficulty learning because of this torture. Mrs. Orr would yell at me and hit me hard on the hands and on my desktop with her ruler. She would also call me stupid. It was my first year of school, and it proved to be a challenging year. For a long time, I believed that I was stupid.

As a young child, being bullied by my elementary school teacher and students, I realized that I was different from the other children, even at the age of six. I realized later, not then, that I was born a medium and empath. Later in life however, I started to develop myself and realized that I am in fact uniquely gifted. This ability as a young child caused me to not fit into the norm. This ability made it even more difficult to understand myself as a child, never mind as an adult. I was bullied during my elementary years by this teacher and other students. It was like going to a torture chamber every day. I did not tell anyone—not even my mother.

I was a very misunderstood youngster. I also told no one about my abilities except my mother. Teachers saw the bullying and let it happen. I was put into a "learning resources" class when I was in grade one. However, teachers back then did not understand me. I realized later in life through my own discovery that I was mildly dyslexic. It made learning in school difficult because the teachers failed to understand me and how I learned. Therefore, my learning disorder helped fuel the bullying because I was different from everyone else. I had trouble reading because I could not focus on what was in front of me. I let my mind slip away and would daydream.

With all my clair senses, growing up was difficult. I would daydream often and found it difficult to concentrate when Spirit was around. My vibration was low, and therefore, I attracted low vibrations to me. The bullying affected my entire adult life and was a huge emotional blockage. It was not until later in my adult life that I started to release these blocks. Bullying is not just someone physically hurting you. It is emotional abuse as well. It develops into a life-long situation of despair if not dealt with. It is emotional damage that tears apart your self-esteem. It can take years, even a lifetime, to rebuild. It makes you feel worthless, different, and helpless. It isolates you from society. Some people react to it by internalizing it and end up with anxiety, depression, weight issues, OCD, or other types of "control" disorders. It fuels negative emotions and can cause severe psychological trauma, among other symptoms.

Being bullied shaped me into who I am today, and as a result, I had to learn to reprogram myself out of a victim mentality. I felt helpless and hopeless from being bullied. It was like my voice did not matter. I remember a boy named Jason punching me so hard in the stomach that I could barely breathe. I would go on to receive this weekly treatment from Jason for over five years. I did not report this. Some people would see it happen and would not do anything about it. I was also teased by the girls in my class. These girls would try to beat me up simply because I was different. I remember them bullying me because I was the tallest and skinniest in class, so they called me "the tree." I was thin, too thin. I refrained from eating because I was sad and because of being traumatized by these back-street bullies. Having an eating disorder at such a young age set the tone for my entire life. Can bullying cause an eating disorder? The answer is yes, it can, and it did with me. I remember these back-street bullies getting other kids together to try to beat me up. I was a fast runner back then, and I would run home as quickly as I could to safety. I would tell no one about this, not even my siblings.

Once elementary school ended, I gained happiness, but I did not have my power. My power was stolen from me in elementary school by these bullies. I remember feeling helpless, unsafe, insecure, and alone. I know the effects remained with me until I released these emotional blockages. The bullying which I endured severely affected me. I doubted myself and had trouble trusting people. The bullies who tortured me as a young child were never confronted, and I never dealt with the situation. I was living with the damage to my self-esteem. These lingering effects did not go away just because I grew up. I have moved on by simply writing my story. I want to help others who have been bullied find their power and the strength to move on with their lives. I was never able to confront my bullies. However, by writing my story and addressing how much pain the bullying had caused me has helped me to heal. I also believe in karma.

Chapter Two- Pandora's Box

Legend states that Pandora was sent a curse, a box that she was prohibited from opening. As soon as she was left alone, she opened the box, and everything subsequently went wrong. Pandora's box is something that generates many complicated problems. I have my own Pandora's box, my life, my storm, my fury. For me, Pandora was not just a box full of chaos, it was a box which held my hidden secrets. This book is my Pandora's box of secrets. Previously, I would lock it shut and tell no one. Little did I know, my life was like a ticking time bomb waiting to go off. I would be given a virtual key to this cursed box labeled Pandora.

I learned to put up with the bullying through my elementary school years until I moved schools to go to Junior high school. Entering Grade 7 proved to be the place for the bullying to end. I made new friends. They were unique friends who liked to talk about Spirit just like me. I played the Ouija board (spirit board) with them, trying to channel spirits of the dead. A Ouija board is a board with the letters of the alphabet written on it. It is used to ask questions which are thought to be answered by the spirits of dead people. It fueled my creative ability. We would also play with my newly acquired tarot cards for fun. These tarot cards were given to me by my eldest sister as a gift. This is something that I still cherish today. It made me realize that I was unique in a beautiful sort of way. I was exceptionally creative. I started to play the clarinet and joined the band at school. I played the lead in this band. It helped to increase my confidence. The people who had previously bullied me faded into the woodwork and were never seen by me again.

After the bullying stopped, I thought that my life was on the upswing. The back-street bullies fell by the wayside and left the scene. Grade 7 was the best year of my life. I made new friends, and it was glorious. My vibration was rising. However, I still had emotional blockages from the past, vibrations which had not been healed. That summer, I was sad to leave school because I loved it so much. Then my grandfather died. Our family needed to move to the country to a farm in Alberta, where my grandparents lived. I was just starting to find my way with new friends when my father told me we were moving to the country. I had been a city girl, after all. I remember just having gained my independence by riding the city buses and going to friends' houses on my own. I felt like my troubles were a thing of the past. Therefore, I was devastated and scared to leave my city home.

That summer in the country was lonely and chaotic for us, trying to get settled into this new way of living. I was terrified and in fear mode, which is the lowest on the emotional guidance scale you can get. It sent my vibration plummeting to the ground. I would have to take a school bus. The thought of this haunted me. The old farmhouse in which my grandparents John and Mary had lived was old and full of spirits. I knew my mother Lena had the gift of mediumship just like me, and later, she would tell me that she saw my Grandpa John's spirit in the basement of this farmhouse. I was still afraid of spirit back then and did not want to move to this haunted farmhouse.

During that summer, I was sent to stay with a family friend named Cassy for a weekend. She lived on her own and was having a party. I am sure my parents were not aware that there was a party, otherwise, they would not have let me go. My parents were very protective of me. They trusted Cassy. We had become close friends. At this party I was introduced to alcohol for the first time. I was only 12. At the party, I met a man named Paul. He was older. He was about twenty years of age. Paul was intrigued by me. I remember being at the stage where I had only dreamed about my first kiss. That was my dream, nothing else. Being as young as I was, kissing was what I wanted, just like in the fairy tale Cinderella, where the prince kisses Cinderella for the first time. It was a dream I wanted, to be kissed for the first time. Paul caught my attention, gave me a drink, and then dragged me into a bedroom. Everything happened quickly.

Everyone was in the living room, and no one saw us leave. Paul asked me to go with him. I started to walk out of the room, then Paul grabbed my arms and dragged me into the bedroom. I tried hard to get loose. Both of my arms were holding on to the walls of the hallway. At the end of this long hallway lay a room of torture. I tried to stop Paul from dragging me to the place where he intended to rape me. I was scared. I remember not being able to use my voice. This was just like when I was being bullied. I felt powerless. That is what I had learned from being bullied—that I was helpless.

As we entered the room, he threw me on the bed, took off my clothes and raped me. As he was raping me, he told me that if I screamed or moved, he would get me pregnant. I did not move. I screamed inside my mind. The thought ran across my mind, "Oh my God, is this happening to me?" I was bleeding, so he dragged me into the bathroom and bathed me. I was terrified, so he fed me drugs. These drugs came in a little package, and until this day, I do not know what they were or how they affected me. I had never taken drugs before in my life. All I know is that I continued to drink heavily that night and told no one about what had happened. He raped me again later that night.

The night became a blur, and I felt that the rape was my fault. I remember Paul still being there the next morning, and when he left, he kissed me goodbye. I never saw or heard from him again. I thought that if I told anyone they would say, "Yes, you are to blame for not screaming." I did not learn to use my voice through most of my adult life. It stems from me being bullied which stems from the vibrations at birth. I remember going home that next day after the weekend was over, and I took a bath trying to wash the rape off my body. My mother knew something was wrong, but I brushed it off as nothing. She screamed at me while I was in the tub and said: "Karen, what is wrong with you, are you ok?" I angrily replied, "I am fine, Mother." It was out-of-the ordinary behavior for me to take a bath in the middle of the day. I would spend the next few weeks worrying about whether I was pregnant. It haunted me to think I could be having a child in such a terrifying way.

Growing up, I started to think that it had not been rape, that it was just an unfortunate incident. I blocked the memories from my mind and could not remember the bath, the drugs, or the alcohol. I only remembered the kiss after. I knew in my soul that I had been raped, but I could not honestly remember the entire event—these were stored inside the Pandora's box until years later. I was afraid of people and how to use my voice. After being bullied, I became accustomed to people pushing me around, so I let them. I did not use my voice. I was frightened, so terrified that I spent my entire adulthood telling no one except my best friend that I had been raped.

Rape is a topic that most people do not want to talk about. However, the truth of the matter is that talking about it releases the power of the incident. Many people have been raped, something that nobody should ever have to go through. The rapist stole my virginity from me and my innocence. I was torn, broken, and tattered. I went through my teen years telling no one else my story and forgetting about this rape entirely. As I got older, I remember telling a few boyfriends about the rape because I was afraid of having sex. I thought if I told them then they would be more sensitive to my issues around intimacy and sexual activity. I did not realize that I grew up not being in my power. I was playing the victim. When you are not in control, you are not in your true self. There's power in standing up for your worth. There's power in defining and owning what you want—and not being afraid of what other people think or say. I let people walk all over me during the most crucial part of my development. It created trauma for me that I hid away.

I remember that after I was raped, I started to eat in an out-of-control fashion. Before that, I was always too skinny. My doctors had been concerned that I was too thin during my entire elementary school year. They were so concerned that they put me on a special diet to fatten me up. The special diet to fatten me up did not work. Then, after the rape, I started to eat. I began to fill out, and I have been preoccupied with weight loss ever since. It was not until my soul journey that I realized that I use food as a coping mechanism because my power had been taken away from me. Even today, I try to gain my power back to the best of my ability.

I believe that victims of sexual abuse as a child are far more likely to become obese adults. Early trauma is so damaging that it can disrupt a person's entire mental health as it did with me. The bullying and rape were so traumatizing they caused me to have an eating disorder that I continue to work through. I ate because of my emotions. Looking back, I remember discussing the issue of weight with my friends. We concluded that being overweight protected me from men. For the most part, it worked. I was always too heavy, and I started to choose the wrong sort of man. Being raped taught me that I was not worth being loved. I remember the kiss that I received from my rapist. All I had wanted was to be loved. The way it happened was terrifying, and the kiss haunts me to this day. All I wanted was to have a first kiss with good intentions of soul love. I have now come to understand that after my rape, my weight was not the only thing that would consume me.

I can now understand that I, too, was bipolar, along with my mother, undiagnosed and unaware. I was unaware and I would not find out until I was 48 years of age. Bipolar is hereditary and can be brought on by trauma and grief. The rape caused the onset of the bipolar disorder. I can acknowledge that, as a young girl, I would have such euphoria one moment and utter despair the next. Since the day I was raped, I grew up with this emotional roller coaster. It has been a nightmare. Your risk of mental illness further increases if the family member with the condition is a close relative. That means if your parent has bipolar disorder, you have a higher chance of developing it. Environmental factors such as abuse, mental stress, a "significant loss," or some other traumatic event may also contribute to or trigger bipolar disorder.

Undiagnosed bipolar disorder started unknowingly after my rape. I remember going through massive ups and downs and crying a lot. It was the summer that I found my life turned upside down. I was starting to drink my father's homemade wine, which was as close to moonshine as you can get. Cassy would take me out to the bars, and we would go drinking. I remember going to see Cassy on weekends, and she would dress me up to look older than I was. I drank back then because I thought that it was what I was supposed to do. It was a coping technique that I used as a 13-year-old in a trauma state. I drank and overate food. It did not help the fact that bipolar disorder was exploding inside of me, waiting to come out.

I had a lot to deal with back then. I had to deal with all my emotions and my trauma from the rape. After a traumatic ordeal, it is natural to feel frightened, sad, anxious, and disconnected. It can sometimes seem that you can never get over what happened or feel normal again. By reaching out for support, and developing new coping skills, you can overcome the issue and move on with your life. I believe I had developed PTSD and was not aware. I disconnected and did not feel my emotions regarding my rape and the bullying. I shut them into Pandora's box for safekeeping. I would go on with life and continue to use my coping mechanisms and to shut out the feelings that I had. I told no one about my darkest secrets. I stored them all into this virtual Pandora's box and locked it up.

I remember that after I was raped, I felt numb and uncontrolled emotionally. I started to cope with the situation by drinking my dad's homemade wine with my girlfriends. I told no one of that horrid time except for my best friend because I was ashamed that I did not scream. I was always ashamed after that, so I hid it from everyone else. I was worried I was pregnant with my rapist's baby. I worried for weeks after. I was terrified at the thought. As it turned out I was not pregnant. But shortly afterwards I developed mono. Paul- the rapist—gave me mono. He would have been sick for weeks before he arrived at Cassy's house that night. I remember people at the party making a fuss over the fact that he was feeling better.

Mononucleosis is known as the kissing disease. It is contracted through saliva. I remember only wanting to sleep when I had mono, until one day my mom pulled my exhausted butt out of bed and took me to the doctors. As you can well imagine, my mother was livid with me. I managed to lie and tell her that I was drinking out of someone else's drinking glass at lunch time. The lie worked. I remember feeling so out of control. I wanted to take my frustrations and anger out on someone. Back then I did not realize I was angry. I can tell you the emotions I was feeling were certainly anger, rage, and resentment.

I fell into a dark space after I was raped, much like a "psychedelic rabbit hole," which is a journey that is particularly strange, problematic, difficult, complex, and chaotic, especially one that becomes progressive as it develops or unfolds. Being undiagnosed with bipolar disorder certainly added to the confusion. Living with bipolar, you experience emotions on a grand scale minute by minute in some cases. With myself, varied emotions occurred even more so with being an empath. Emotions are powerful, indeed. The emotions were so powerful, I stored them inside Pandora's box. Emotions are so powerful that I can feel the energy of Spirit run through me while experiencing them.

After I was raped however, I started to forget about Spirit. I stopped seeing, I stopped believing. I fell into such a depressive state that I was not aware of it. I was barely aware of my own life. I remember buying strawberry wine on weekends with my friends from school. We would hang out behind the school and listen to music and drink the wine which tasted like fruit punch. I would also go fishing by the river with my farming friends from school. We would fish and drink beer—not enough to get into trouble, just enough to ease the pain that I was going through. We would have fun. I carried on like an average teenager, but with my emotions being so escalated from bipolar, it was a nightmare to contain them.

I was battling a lot of different issues at this time. Spirit was the farthest thing from my mind. I was simply surviving. I can tell you that I probably was manic earlier in my life because I showed the symptoms of it throughout various periods. During the emotional highs, I became full of energy and overly excited about life. During the lows, I felt down and empty. Looking back at my life I remember all through my life that I would speak loudly, and very quickly. My family would always comment on it and tell me to quiet down and speak more slowly. This would drive me crazy because that was just how I was. No one actually thought I was mentally ill.

The year after I was raped, I started to develop severe allergies. I became allergic to everything. What I now understand is that stress is a significant cause of allergies. It is known that emotions trigger the release of many chemicals in the body. Joyous emotions produce healing chemicals, while negative emotions dump disease-causing chemicals into our system. It is amazing to me to realize what stress can do to the body.

I believe that emotions are everything, whether good or bad. They can affect your health severely if you let them. My emotions were in turmoil, and I was numb. I repressed all my emotions and went on with my life. I went on in a dysfunctional way. However. I was an emotional basket case. The rape sent me into such turmoil it sent out negative vibrations. What you think about, you attract. I was thinking such negative, depressive thoughts for years ever since I was in elementary school that it brought negative events. The negative vibration would continue for years.

I can understand now that the negative vibration led me to make terrible decisions. After I was raped, Cassy took me away to the big city for the weekend as she had before, and my parents let her, thinking that it was fine. This weekend was different because the rape forced me to grow up. I had turned 13 and I thought I was a little adult. When I arrived in the city, Cassy dressed me up and took me to the bar and I met a fellow named George. George took a liking to me. I was only 13 and George was 18 plus years of age. Cassy told George that I was 18. I chatted with George and had drinks.

Later. we went back to George's place and George and I started to kiss, then we had sex. I thought it was terrible considering all I wanted was to be a princess as you read in fairy tales. However, George was much different from Paul. Paul raped me and George had sex with me, a much different story.

Sex was horrible for me. It brought back a feeling of terror. I remember crying after and George did not know what to do but he was gentle, and we cuddled. I knew inside that it was wrong what I was doing but I felt obliged. That is what the rape did to me. Looking back now, I can see how terrible the situation really was for me. I remember George calling me a few days later and he was kind and really liked me. When I told him that I was only 13 I was shocked. He told me that he could never see me again. I was devastated because all I really wanted was love.

Going through my teen years was tumultuous. It was full of chaos, as seen through an emotional perspective. I had a few boyfriends whom I dated but nothing significant. What I can understand now is that the rape set off my bipolar disorder and it caused me to be unbalanced throughout the years. I left home at the early age of 17. I was afraid of moving on to a new life after high school, and this triggered undiagnosed mania. It was the start of chaos for me. I look back and ask myself this question: why did I choose to not tell anyone about my rape? After all, I grew up in a loving household with a loving mother and father and four supportive siblings. We grew up with no abuse and with high family values. I told no one because I was afraid. I was afraid of bothering my family for something that I thought was my fault. I can now understand that it was not my fault. However, I went through most of my adult life believing differently. It caused me to seek out something that was not there. I wanted to find love. I wanted the feeling of a first kiss, a romantic soul kind of love that one can imagine only in fairy tales and chick flick movies. I would go out partying with my friends and drink and have casual sex with men whom I barely knew. It was the norm for my friends and me. It is what we did.

I decided to move to the city to take my hairstylist training. During this part of my life, I started to date men who were bad for me. I would sleep with men on first dates to get them to like me and love me. I was searching for love in all the wrong places. This behavior is evidence of an emotional failing of some sort. I had to search for why I did this, and it used to bother me. I now understand that I did this because of my bipolar. According to Everyday Health, manic, abrupt and reckless sexual behaviors, and significantly increased sex drive are quite common. This hypersexual behavior is often a warning sign of a manic episode.

Promiscuity in women, casual sexual behavior, is no longer viewed quite as negatively as it used to be. However, I do know that I was promiscuous not only because I was in bipolar mania throughout periods of my life, but also due to the fact that I had been raped at such a young age. Rape is about power and control, not sex, and can hurt self-esteem and well-being. According to my online research, victims frequently react to rape by pursuing multiple sexual encounters to find someone who will make them feel safe. This is especially true of those who have experienced childhood sexual abuse.

I remember going out with my friends to bars, one in particular was called 'Rock City'. We would go out and meet men, go back to their place and have sex. Most of the time they were 'one-night stands'. If they actually called us after, this was a rare occurrence. I shake my head at how many men I slept with in my young adult years. It resembled the HBO series "Sex and the City," in which Carrie and her friends frequented bars in their quest to meet men, serving as a reference point for the situation. This was my life. I can look back and understand that I only wanted someone to love me. I did not contract any sexual disease. That is a blessing to me. I also met guys who were kind and wanting the same thing as I did. What I have learned however, is that any relationship worth having needs to develop over time. Sex is actually something that should be held off until you really get to know someone. That is what I have learned in my later years. Back then I had no idea how sacred the art of making love to someone could be.

As time went on, I used food, alcohol, and shopping as coping mechanisms. I was on an emotional rollercoaster all of my adult life. It was what I knew. I started to become engrossed in a new life of using credit and making my own money. I spent all my hard-earned money on shopping. One of the most common symptoms of bipolar is impulsive and irrational spending. It was a significant issue for me, and to some extent, it still is. I had every credit card you can imagine. Back then each individual store had their own credit card. I had them all. I lived close to the world's largest indoor shopping mall.

I racked up around $30,000.00 worth of debt. Soon the creditors came calling because I found it too much to keep up with the payments. I remember paying $250 for rent back then, which was a deal. Thus I had a fair share of money to be able to pay these creditors. It still was not enough. I bit off more than I could chew. Around this time, I was in a car accident and was injured. The ambulance came and took me to the hospital. A friend told me to contact a lawyer because the accident was not my fault. As it turned out, I received enough from the accident to pay off my debt and to buy myself a new vehicle. I cancelled my credit cards and did not rack them up again. Little did I know that my Pandora's box of secrets was something that was festering inside of me.

Chapter Three- The Soul's Calling

As long as I can remember I was interested in creating, building, and achieving. I had developed the entrepreneurial spirit, and I soon started my own business doing hairstyling. I became addicted to my career. I finished my hairstylist training and started my makeup training. It was a fun time for me, and I kept focused on work. However, this did not stop me from going out and finding love in all the wrong places during my time off. I remember working very hard on my career during this time. I applied for a student loan to go to makeup school in Hollywood, California where I would train to be a special effects makeup artist. I created a special effects makeup on a model. My submission to the makeup academy was enough to win a scholarship. I would attend professional makeup school where I would be able to do all types of makeup, especially special effects makeup on actors for movies, television, and special events. I remember being scared to go. It was then that my mother told me of her premonition. She stated that I would meet someone in my hometown and get married. That is precisely what happened.

I met a fellow named Malcom on my mother's birthday at the local horse races. We met, and I married him two months later. I understand now that it was something that felt safe at the time. I needed something to keep me from going to Hollywood because I was too scared to go. I did not realize that at the time, but I now know it to be true. I remember weeks before the wedding day, Malcom said to me just before bed, "You don't want to marry me, do you? But you are afraid to call it off because your parents have paid for the wedding already." I looked at Malcom and simply brushed it off. The truth was Malcom was bang on. I could not turn back and tell my parents that the wedding was off. They had invested so much money into our wedding I would have felt ashamed. So, the wedding went as scheduled. The morning of the wedding I was so nervous because I knew I was doing the wrong thing.

Just before the wedding I asked my bridesmaid if she would sneak a beer into my room where I was getting ready, in order to calm my nerves. She refused. I was so angry with her for not obliging. After all, being a bride, you are queen for the day and my needs were not being met. When the limousine which held me, my mother, father, and bridesmaid arrived at the church I noticed that Malcom and his best man were also just arriving. I found out later that they had been at the local bar. I was so angry when I found that out, but I pushed it aside and went on with my wedding day. The wedding night was a bust because Malcom drank too much and ended up passing out on me. I was awake and enjoyed the champagne and appetizers that the hotel had provided for us in our luxury honeymoon suite, with hot tub all by myself. I enjoyed the night while Malcom slept.

Our relationship turned out to be rocky. He was a functioning alcoholic, and I was not. I used alcohol for fun and as a mood enhancer, but I have never abused it. Malcom started to abuse me emotionally. The abuse was never physical, but it certainly was mental. To distract myself, I started my mobile hair and makeup company. I helped pioneer the mobile beauty industry in Canada. Soon after, I combined forces with Canada's largest mobile hair company at the time. It was during this partnership that I gained valuable business knowledge about the industry. The partnership did not last long however, but the training I received while we were together proved to be invaluable throughout my years in business. Business fueled my passion for many years until I had my breakdown much later in my story.

I was married to Malcom for just over two years when it just became too much for me to handle emotionally. I divorced Malcom, and shortly after, I was scheduled for my first makeup competition. That morning my mother called me to tell me to "break a leg" as they do in show business, to wish me good luck. This was something my mother had never said to me before. At this makeup competition, I did just that. I broke my leg just before they announced I was the first-place winner. It was another premonition of my mother's. I broke my leg so badly that I needed surgery. As a result, I have a 12-inch metal plate in my leg. I remember my mother telling me, "You picked this time to listen to me." It was not a good time for me. However, I dusted myself off and carried on. I became a workaholic. I understand now that I used work as a coping mechanism. I became highly successful in my career. I went on to date other men and continued being promiscuous, but Spirit was trying to take me over. I met three women who were friends, all ministers of different denominations. We became close. They took me under their wing. These three wise women gave me comfort and helped me to realize that there was more to life than dating men. Several years later, I met a man named Samuel.

My life was very unbalanced. I was unknowingly living with bipolar. I was addicted to running my business. My vibration and alignment were all over the place because of the escalated emotions I experienced. I lived my life moment to moment until I met Samuel. Samuel was different from any man that I had ever dated. He was balanced and had his life together. I did my best to keep balanced but with the downfalls of undiagnosed bipolar, it proved to be complicated. Samuel and I dated for several years before I decided to move in with him. My mother told me not to move in with Samuel because he would never marry me. She proved to be correct yet again.

Samuel and I had dated for three years when his mother died and went into the nonphysical. Her funeral was set for the same day I was to go to a crucial meeting. This meeting was for the World Track and Field Games. I was to be a lead makeup artist for their closing ceremonies, and I needed to pick an assistant. If I did not attend this meeting, it would jeopardize my opportunity to participate. I chose not to go to this meeting, but instead to be with Samuel in his time of grief. Samuel talked me into going to this meeting after his mother's funeral. Samuel agreed to go with me for emotional support as I, too, was grieving his mother's passing because she had been an essential part of our lives together as a couple.

I remember talking to a friend named Noelia about this grief. She was of First Nation descent. Her insight into this death was that the Great Spirit would bring someone into my life who would be a vibrational match to the person who has passed on. That intrigued me. We went to the funeral and soon after, left for the meeting and to pick out my assistant for these games. It was at the meeting that a lady popped up her hand and agreed to be my assistant. It was good enough for me. She introduced herself to Samuel and me. Her name was Joyce, the same name as Samuel's mother. Joyce was 20 years older than I. She and I became best friends over the years. I called Joyce my angel friend. She was there for me every step of my life after that. Joyce taught me all about the Law of Attraction. We would study this New Age concept together, and we went to Law of Attraction retreats to try to gain perspective on this manifestation law.

When it came to my business, Joyce would help me at any opportunity. We drank champagne together and solved the world's most significant issues. Then Joyce's son died, it changed her as she had found Spirit. She was introduced to a spiritual church, which became a new outlet to fuel her passion for life again and later mine. It was at this time that I was working on my business trying to expand my mobile company to go to nationwide franchising. I would do hair and makeup for television, movies, and other special events. It was my passion, and I was great at it. When I wanted to franchise, the only thing that was holding me back was that I did not have a physical space to house this mobile company. We required a headquarters, and the only way I knew how to do that was to get a business partner. So I did. I sold 30% of my mobile company, then called In Motion Style Group, to a lady named Sally who was the same age as me. I sold it for $40,000.00. I put most of the money back into the business to expand it. We purchased a 5000 square foot salon and spa. I renovated it with no help from others. I developed my makeup academy and my own brand of hair, makeup, and skincare. It was a dream come true.

We were working on the procedures and policies to get the business ready to franchise when Sally, my business partner, walked out on the business because she had just had a baby and could not cope. My payroll and bills every month accumulated to $20,000.00 plus. I would have to make that up through services every month just to break even. I had bitten off more than I could chew. I became so stressed that I became physically ill. I thought it was the flu. I did not go to the doctor at first. I progressively got sicker and finally saw the doctor who told me to go to the hospital. I ended up in the emergency ward of the hospital. The doctors there also thought it was the flu. They thought I was wasting their time.

Then the results of the blood tests came back. I was very sick, so sick the doctors did not understand how I was functioning. They first thought that I had a burst appendix. As it turned out, my organs—my kidneys and my bladder—were slowly shutting down. I was dying. I felt like I was having a near death experience. They found a grapefruit-sized abscess on my colon that was spitting poisons into my body. They put me on antibiotics and wanted to perform surgery once the antibiotics started to work. In a few days, I started to feel better. I remember being marked with a black marker on my stomach where they would put the colostomy bag that I would have to wear.

I was so distraught. The doctors also thought that I had cancer. This stressed me out. Once they figured out that I did not have cancer, they scheduled the surgery. I was put on a gurney, and an orderly came to wheel me away when suddenly the nurse as the station received a call to say the surgery was cancelled. Soon after, three surgeons came into my room and asked me how I was feeling. I told them I was feeling great as the antibiotics had kicked in. They chose to use a new technique in which they would go in with a needle into my lower back and drain the abscess with a tube. It worked beautifully. They arranged to have home care nurses come check on me daily for about six weeks.

I recovered from this life-changing experience, but it transformed my world completely. I understand now that it was my dis-ease fueling this medical trauma. That is why it is so essential to understand your emotions and keep them on the high side of the emotional scale. Disease, disorders, and ailments come from stress being built up over time. For the first time in my life, I had nothing to do but concentrate on myself—no coping mechanisms to be found, not even food because I was put on a special diet. It made me look at life in an entirely different way. I started to realize that what mattered most was not things, or the business, but my life. Life was precious. I had taken it for granted. I started to change the way I lived my life, including how I handled my business.

I started to realize I had had everything I wanted to have in my career, but it wasn't making me happy. I still needed to pay the bills, so I arranged to have an open house for my new In Motion Salon and Spa. It was grand in scale. It had all the bells and whistles. I had even arranged for media to be present. At this open house, I met a friend from high school. She was so impressed with my achievements. She said, "You must be thrilled!" It was then that I looked at her and, without hesitation, said, "No, I hate it." I realized then that my life had changed. I decided to make a bold, life-changing move.

Soon after, I spoke to Sally, my business partner who had walked out on me. We agreed that she would buy the business from me, and that I would take over the contracts located in the senior facilities. We had three beauty salons which were located in senior facilities. I would still have shares in the salon and spa part of the company. That was for my retirement fund. In the end, Sally walked away from the business, and I had to go and clean up the mess. She left me with all the business debt, leaving me no retirement money and no legacy from the franchising. The business partner she had found to look after the business ended up being a drug addict who spent all of the business' funds. It was heartbreaking. I had worked so hard to achieve my dream, and I honestly thought Sally was going to flourish with the legacy that I had left her. I realized then that she needed the missing link to make it work. That missing link was me.

I cleaned up the mess Sally left behind the best I could, but I was left with a $40,000.00 debt. I did my best to gradually pay this off. What I can understand now is that when you are living with an undiagnosed mental illness, the decisions that you make are not always the correct ones. My undiagnosed bipolar disorder made achieving success difficult. It also blocked me from using my intuition and leading a healthy soul filled life.

I thought I had been living a happy life with Samuel while running my seniors facility salons. What I did not realize was how unhappy my relationship was with Samuel. We never kissed as couples do in romantic comedies. This made me sad. There were never passionate kisses which was something I had wanted. Despite this fact, I still wanted to marry Samuel because he became a pivotal part of my life and was one of my best friends. I would communicate my needs to Samuel, but he would not accommodate me. Samuel would not talk about emotions although I was starting to be good at it. We often clashed.

I spent the next two years being in and out of hospital. I would get sick, and the doctors were not entirely sure what to do or what was wrong with me. Then they did exploratory surgery on me, and I underwent a full hysterectomy. I could no longer have children which was something I had considered at different times in my life. I remember back when I had asked

Samuel if he wanted to have children. We were vacationing in British Columbia. He abruptly told me to stop talking about it because it was ruining his vacation. From then on, we never talked about having children or of marriage. This made me sad, so I chose to focus on expanding my business.

After my hysterectomy I became engrossed in the Law of Attraction. Joyce and I became closer friends. I had become interested in Spirit once again, and I started to regularly see psychics. It was the start of the days when I would seek out advice on the future. I would never want to know about Samuel, though, because I knew in my heart that it was not the right match for me. That made me sad because he was my best friend. The truth was that I wanted more from a relationship; I wanted soul love. Our relationship was like putting a square peg into a round hole—it simply did not fit. Samuel did not believe in soul growth or even spiritual mediums for that matter. We lived common-law for 13 years. His house became my house. In Alberta, Canada, the laws for common-law relationships are recognized in the court of law. I felt safe for the first time in my life. We had a large yard and a garden, something that I loved. There was a double garage to store all my products for the shops. It was my home sweet home.

There was only one problem. Samuel was always afraid that I would take him for half of his money. He wanted a prenuptial agreement even though there were no signs of getting married. So I arranged to get this prenuptial agreement compiled by my lawyer stating that if I left, I would not take the house, nor would I take Samuel's money that he had saved. If we didn't have the prenuptial agreement, then half of Samuel's savings and half of the house would be mine if we split up. In love and honor, I quickly compiled the agreement, and Samuel was to sign this with his lawyer. However, this never happened. The lawyer sent me the final bill for the agreement, and Samuel was told to get it signed with his lawyer to finalize this part of our lives. Samuel then realized there was no need to go any further and chose not to sign the agreement. He had started to trust me on a deeper level. I had no intention of leaving, nor did I ever consider taking his house or his money. I was, after all, an independent woman. I put money into the home because it was my home as well. I thought Samuel and I would spend our entire lives together. Little did I know Spirit and my bipolar disorder would change that.

After having a full hysterectomy, I was in full-blown menopause and was also unknowingly living with bipolar. This became challenging for me. I was unaware of what was really going on. There was a tornado deep inside waiting to destroy my life. I refused to take hormones which would have helped me. I had no idea back then how the mixture of being in menopause and being bipolar would soon destroy my life. After a few years passed, I became uneasy with my life. I decided to grow my three beauty salons into more. I grew them into 15 beauty salons, all of them in seniors facilities. It made my heart sing. I started to become a workaholic again. Samuel forced me to be balanced, and it drove me crazy. I would ensure that I was at home every night to make him dinner. It was our routine. When he worked nights, I took that as my night off from my wifely duties, and I worked from home.

I was engrossed in building up my new company to become a franchise. However, I was lonely while living with Samuel. I had the two dogs that Joyce, my angel friend, had given me. Joyce could not look after them any longer because of her lifestyle. So after years of dog sitting, we were permitted to keep the dogs. They were my babies—Buddy and Korky, two Bichon poodles. I could not have children, so I poured my love into these four-legged animals which brought so much joy and happiness into my life.

I started to make good money which I would rapidly spend. I was earning over $350,000.00 Canadian per year. There was no mortgage to pay, so with all the extra money, I chose to travel. Then I realized my mother's illness of arthritis was hereditary. I started to have such bad arthritis that I could barely walk for days at a time, and I would have to cancel days at work. This made it impossible to travel at that time. According to Spiritual Energy Medical Theory, what is behind arthritis is anger at yourself. It is a theory that every ailment you have is caused by emotions of some kind. I did not realize that I was angry. However, deep inside I was. I had stored my emotions inside of myself for so long that I was unaware that they even existed. With my arthritis being so severe, I started to think I would be in a wheelchair in a few years—it was that bad. I decided to travel while I could. Travelling proved to be difficult due to my arthritis so I decided to see a naturopathic doctor. He changed my world. On the advice of the naturopath, I went on a cleanse and started to eat according to my blood type. We eliminated all the foods that I was sensitive and allergic to.

Miraculously, this regimen totally resolved my arthritis, but I was in denial about my anger and kept it inside Pandora's box.

With my arthritis in check, I traveled all over with Samuel. We went to Europe and traveled to England. We went all over the Caribbean islands: Antigua, Barbados, Colombia, Dominican Republic, Martinique, Grenada, Guyana, Haiti, Honduras, Jamaica, Aruba, Curaçao, Saint Marten, Nicaragua, Guatemala, Panama, Saint Kitts, Saint Lucia, Saint Vincent and the Grenadines, Trinidad and Tobago, the British Virgin Islands, Cayman Island, Puerto Rico, St. Thomas, The Bahamas, and my favorite to date—Turks and Caicos Islands. Samuel and I would cruise the Caribbean islands on cruise lines which were so luxurious it makes me feel at peace just thinking about it. On these cruise lines, there were casinos. I had become accustomed to going to casinos with my parents and Samuel. Life was perfect, or so I thought. What I did not realize was missing was pure soul love. I yearned for that.

I remember coming home from these cruises and being so unhappy. I was suffering from destination addiction. I understand now that I was so unhappy spiritually speaking that I felt a need to always travel and leave my home life. Samuel and I loved islands, and the closest thing we had to Islands near Alberta, Canada, is Vancouver Island, British Columbia. We travelled to Vancouver Island over 20 times just to get away. It helped keep our relationship alive. But deep down I knew that Samual was not meant to be mine. I knew it in my soul but was lying to myself, but I continued living with Samual for years after.

Times were great until my mother became ill. She was only 72, and her arthritis medicine had stopped working. The medication caused her to have liver failure and heart disease. I have never been an advocate for any big pharmaceutical companies because of this experience. On those television advertisements where they say the medication can cause particular side effects, well, it happened for my mother. My mother's health started to fail. She required a walker to walk, and just like that, everyone around me was aging. My mother and father would start to fall and break bones. It was a nightmare for me, as I was in and out of hospitals all the time taking care of them. I was lucky that I had a business so I could leave my place of work when

I needed to. It was a lot to take on when I was not mentally healthy myself. The reality is that aging is a fact of life, and it affects everyone involved.

I was the main care provider for my parents when they started to age. It took its toll on my mental health. I remember one day when my mother was very sick and needed an ambulance, I was not around to help. Samual and I went out for dinner with friends. I received a phone call from my siblings that I needed to go and help immediately. I was expected to drop my plans and help my parents. It was a very frustrating and exhausting time, both mentally and physically. I had to juggle my business, home and spiritual life while taking care of my parents. It proved to be overwhelming and challenging to say the least—something that I was not prepared for.

During the time when my parents were aging and needing more care, I worked in senior facilities where aging and death was the norm. My dear clients who became friends would die on a weekly basis. I remember not being able to keep staff because their clients would die, and it would be difficult for them emotionally. As hairdressers, these clients became our friends. Around this time, my close friend Laura died. She was the same age as I was. It was difficult, and she, too, was unhappy in her life. She was so unhappy that she committed suicide. In a way, I was jealous she was able to leave, and that I had to stay. This was the depressive state that would wash over me like rain every now and then.

I felt everybody was leaving me. My parents were my best friends. They meant the world to me, and they were starting to age very quickly. My baby dogs were aging. One dog started to become blind, and the other had arthritis. These were challenging times for me. Samuel's knee started to act up, and his temper started to flare up. He was miserable, and so was I. We had scheduled two vacations on luxury cruise lines to the Caribbean Islands in the Fall and Winter of 2012. However, life was starting to take a turn for the worse. I started to go to the casino with Samuel weekly. I struggled emotionally. I covered this up by going to the casino. Samuel relentlessly exerted his dominance over me, restricting my interactions with friends, dictating my work schedule, and constantly reminding me that the house did not belong to me. His behavior amounted to a heavy burden, taking a toll on my emotional well-being. Everyone was started to get ill at the same time. My oldest sister had a massive stroke and ended up in a wheelchair, and she had been my support. It did not help my mental state as I was taking care of my parents too. It was simply too much for me to manage.

I had previously thought that my life would be a fairy tale. I thought I would be married and have children with Samuel. Instead, as time went on, we grew further and further apart. It was then that I started to gamble all my spending money away. Gambling was starting to control my life, and it was a struggle. Back then, I had no idea why. I even once went to a Gamblers Anonymous meeting only to find that it was closed when I arrived. I never went back. I was too ashamed. I figured that I could solve my gambling problem by myself, and I did, the hard way. I chose the expensive way, through trial and error. I remember telling friends about my gambling, trying to understand why I was acting out in this addictive way. I had never had an addiction prior to this, and our family did not have these issues. What I came to understand was that gambling helped me cope with the sad life that I was living. Additionally, my bipolar disorder helped fuel the fire, causing my marriage to be unbalanced.

At one point I won $5000.00 at a casino. That was the fuel that activated my addiction. I would spend my time at the dollar machines and maximum bet all the time. Sometimes the maximum bet was $20 per spin. I felt that those were the best machines. They created high adrenaline which fueled me. I would often win $1000 or more, but I wouldn't stop until I won the big win. Once you are in debt by $1000 to $5000, it is difficult to stop until you at least break even. Gambling is a terrible disease, and bipolar, specifically mania, helps to fuel it. What I can now understand from taking the energy psychology workshops is that once you hit that adrenaline high, you always strive to experience that feeling again. When you are bipolar manic, it is like being a kid in a candy store. I was the kid, and the casino was the candy store for me. Gambling was a profoundly serious addiction for me. I had to spend a lot of time soul searching to remedy this.

Addictions can be dangerous, more so than a lot of coping mechanisms. I could control most of my coping mechanisms to a certain extent, like shopping and food, that were borderline addictions for me. Gambling, however, was an absolute addiction. Now I understand that with going untreated with bipolar and splashes of mania, then adding in a gambling addiction, was like adding fuel to the fire. I would gamble whether I was up or down. I kept gambling regardless of the consequences. I continued to gamble even when I knew that the odds were against me. A coping mechanism is something a person does to deal with a difficult situation. An addiction, however, is uncontrollable. I used coping mechanisms when I was faced with stress. I could control these. I could not control my gambling. I managed to control it to a certain extent. However, it was still a large issue for me financially.

A gambling problem can strain your relationships and lead to financial disaster. I consider myself lucky because the addiction did not interfere with my relationship or with work. Nonetheless, it affected my soul. It bothered me that I could not stop gambling. I did my best to stop. I controlled the addiction to a point. What I knew for sure was that I did not want the life that I had. I wanted something much grander. What I did not realize was that my soul was calling me. I felt the urge to connect with spirit and my soul on a deep spiritual level.

Chapter Four- Middle Aged Crazy

I did my best to push my feelings of a spiritual calling aside, and that was to pour my efforts into building my kingdom so I could be happy. That is what I truly wanted, a home of my very own, a husband with a ring on my finger and a spiritually enlightened life. So I did what I knew best, put all my efforts into planning my next business venture. That is where I excelled, in business building. That fall was the start of my business franchising plan. I was to redesign all my salons to look the same with the same procedures and so forth; this proved to be much more complicated than it had first appeared.

During this time, we were scheduled to open salon number 16. It gave me a purpose, and I started to need that in my life, a bigger purpose. I remember going out for a celebration one night with my personnel manager, Heather. It was to celebrate salon number 16. We went to a pub called Sherlock Holmes. It was a pub where there was live music. I remember feeling ugly. I needed to go out and feel pretty, feel alive. Music did that for me. I remember Heather going to the bathroom. While she was gone, a nice-looking Jamaican gentleman appeared. We caught each other's eye, and when we did, we were both mesmerized. I looked at him and prayed to the Great Spirit and said, "Great Spirit, why can't I have a boyfriend like that?" Then just like that, the Jamaican gentlemen appeared in front of me and introduced himself as Jack. We hit it off as if we had been friends forever. I had been to Jamaica, and as a result, we had a lot to chat about. Jack was tall, over 6"2", muscular, and bold looking. He had a way with words and knew exactly what to say. When Heather came back from the bathroom, she thought Jack was an old friend of mine because we hit it off so quickly. There was no thought process in what I did. We exchanged phone numbers, and Jack would text me messages over the next few weeks. Messages like, "Hi baby, how are you today?"

Jack swept me off my feet. Samuel would never have called me baby or sweet talk me. Jack helped me to gain my confidence back and helped me realize what I was missing. I realized that I was missing out on life, and that I was very unhappy with my current situation. I tried to discuss this with Samuel, but he would not discuss it. I started to lose weight and shift my perspective to myself for the first time in my life. At this point, I gambled a lot less. Weeks passed. I decided to leave Samuel. It was a decision that made sense to me. I thought that if I stayed with Samuel, I would never be loved the way I was meant to be loved. I wanted to be fair to Samuel and not stay in a relationship with him when I was not happy. I started to see Jack while I was living with Samuel. Looking back, I believe I was manic then. When you are manic, you make poor decisions and do not care about the outcome.

I remember telling my oldest sister about this situation. She was supportive of me. She was always unconditional with her love. One night during this time, my sister and I decided to bring dinner to Samual at work. As we were driving to Samuel's work, I told my sister everything about Jack. I told her that I loved Jack. While we were driving, my sister phoned Samuel to let him know that we were on our way to drop off his dinner. By mistake my sister did not press the hang-up button. Therefore, our entire conversation was recorded on Samuel's answering machine, including the "I love Jack" comment. All the dirties, everything, how he swept me off my feet and how I wanted to leave Samuel.

I remember Samuel had not told me that he knew of this conversation until weeks later. One night Samuel woke me at about 3 am in a frantic panic, telling me he knew about Jack and me. I was frightened because Samuel was aggressive and distraught. I was afraid for my life. I told Samuel that I wanted to leave him. Samuel made it difficult for me. We had been scheduled to go on a cruise a few weeks down the road. I agreed to still go on the cruise, I did this out of fear, which we know is at the bottom of the vibrational scale, and my vibration was at an all-time low. It was a nightmare. Samuel, who seldom drank, was drinking alcohol like it was water and who was never violent, was angry all the time. Despite what my instincts were telling me, I agreed to give it one more chance with Samuel. I stayed longer than I wanted to. During this time, Samuel became so angry one night that I called the police. It was a terrible situation. During this time, I would still see Jack as a friend. Soon after, Jack left for Jamaica for six months. When I decided to leave Samuel, I chose to leave regardless of whether it worked out for Jack and me. I felt that if Jack can make me feel as good as he did, then there was someone out there who belongs in my heart.

Christmas time was coming in the winter of 2012, and I did not want to leave Samuel during Christmas. I remember going to a therapist around that time. He told me to be careful. People in this situation can become dangerous. I was already scared of Samuel before the therapist said that, and his words made me even more scared to leave Samuel. The vibration around me was extremely negative. I remember wanting to leave Samuel years before. I thought it would kill my parents, so I stayed longer than I should have.

I finally became brave enough to do something that I should have done years before. I planned to leave Samuel on December 27th of 2012. My friend Maple came to my house that morning. I packed up only what we could fit into the vehicle, and I left. I left it all behind. No courts, no lawsuit. I just left. I had scheduled myself to leave for Jamaica that same day for a period of three weeks. Jack had gone there to run his restaurant. I knew that I needed to leave town for a while because Samuel was so desperate to get me to stay it would have been dangerous for me. I left the dogs behind because they were too old to come with me and that broke my heart. They were comfortable with Samuel, and I had nowhere else to keep them. I am sure that I was in shock during this time and undoubtedly manic. I just walked away from my home that I had had for years. As I drove away, my baby dogs were looking out the window. Were they wondering when I would be coming home? My heart was breaking but I had no choice but to leave. It did not make sense to stay in a loveless relationship. I blasted the song playing on my CD player, Beyonce's "All the Single Ladies". I was now a free woman, and I was heading to Jamaica that night. It was a new start filled with freedom and possibilities.

My first stop was my oldest sister's place to drop off some items that she had agreed to store for me. I was supposed to stay with her when I got back from Jamaica, but as her small one bedroom was starting to look like a storage room, it looked less appealing. It was early morning and I waited for my half day of work to start at one of my beauty salons located in a seniors facility. My head felt a bit fuzzy, and my body was filled with adrenaline. I finished unpacking and started to organize my purse for my trip. I did a few more things to organize my sister's house and realized when I went to leave that I had misplaced my credit card. What an ordeal that was! I could not find it anywhere. I had to go to Jamaica without it. I phoned the credit card company. They would send me another one, that I would receive after my trip.

I reluctantly headed out to work. I was planning to have my assistant take care of the business while I was away. I pulled up to work, thanking God for my freedom. I listened to Beyonce's song multiple times. She sings about how he should have put a ring on her finger. I felt empowered. As I went in, I saw clients anxiously waiting to see me. They were excited to hear how the move went, as I told my favorite clients all the gossip about my life. A half day went by quickly. Just before I left, I called my favorite psychic hotline to find out how my life was going to be. This time I get a real winner. She told me that there was no hope for a relationship with Jack. I politely said goodbye to the psychic and absorbed the cost of $75 for a few minutes of psychic consultation. I left the salon still filled with hope but just a little bit less optimistic. I brushed off the feeling that I had made a disastrous mistake and went on with my day.

I dropped off my car to store at my friend's place while I was gone. Time flew by, and my assistant had agreed to drive me to the airport. The thought crossed my mind that I would be alone without Samuel. That was a realization that had not occurred to me previously, that I would be alone until I reached Jamaica. I put on a brave face and wondered how Jack would be when I arrived. He had been difficult on the phone the last time we had spoken. I was wondering what I had done wrong. As I waited for my flight, I took out my regular class ticket out and could not help but wonder how previously I had paid for Jack to fly to Jamaica first class and here I was flying regular class. Nonetheless, I had not been in my right mind at that time to make proper life decisions. At the time it had seemed amusing to buy him a first- class ticket, and I was oblivious to the ramifications.

The flight attendant on the plane was very accommodating when I told her I lost my credit card. She kindly gave me a sandwich. The plane ride was smooth. I had no thoughts of what I had left behind. As we landed in Toronto, I decided to change my clothing. I chose shorts and a cute top so

I would look summer like for Jack when I arrived in Jamaica. We landed in Jamaica, and I headed to customs, thinking, "I am not in Kansas anymore". I was off on an adventure that was very different from my usual way of life. I wondered for a brief moment what I had done. I arrived at customs and realized that I had no idea where I was going. I was supposed to stay with Jack at his hotel. I somehow navigated my way through customs. I am not sure how or why they let me in with such little information. I was living on a "wing and a prayer". As I reached the airport exit, the air hit me. It was hot, very hot. It was a very pleasant change of scenery.

I looked around and saw that Jack was not there. I started to panic; I finally saw him in the distance by the outdoor patio bar. He handed me a shot of tequila. His driver took us to the hotel. I couldn't wait. I was expecting the best of the best. We arrived in Negril. It is a beach resort town. As we pulled into what I expected to be a posh resort, I saw a run-down motel. I was not impressed. I had no choice but to go with the flow. There was a safe in the room and I stored the cash that I had brought. It was a lot, close to $5,000. I did not have a credit card and I was not sure if my debit card would work. Jack saw this and asked me to give him $1500 for a debt he owed to the liquor store so that he could restock his bar. His brown eyes and dark skin melted my heart and I gave in. We went to his restaurant and bar, one that was very typical of the small Caribbean Island. It overlooked the rocky side of the ocean but was not on a sandy beachfront. I was introduced to his employees; they were kind to me. Jack told them that I could order whatever I wanted. That surprised me because I was usually the one who paid.

That night, there was a special dance party featuring Bob Marley songs. "Three little Birds" was playing as I sang out loud and drank my glass of bubbly. The lyrics told me to not "worry about a thing". I finally relaxed. As the song echoed in the air, the realization dawned upon me – a sense of liberation I hadn't felt in years. The DJ, immersed in the rhythmic flow of Bob Marley's tunes, became a catalyst for my newfound freedom, breaking the chains that tethered me to my past relationship with Samuel.

A few days later it was New Years Eve, my favorite time of year. We celebrated with champagne. The next day we rented a vehicle and drove throughout Negril and the outlying area, visiting Jack's friends from various times of his life. The Rastafarians became my favorites, as they appeared particularly interested in me due to my outsider status, as I didn't quite fit into their world. We had great times, and it was a treasure visiting people who actually lived there. We drove with the windows down and the music blasting. One song I remember is "Stayin Alive" by the Bee Gees. These were great memories.

Jack wanted to use my money to stay at a resort while I was there. Resorts were very expensive, and money was going fast the way Jack was spending it. We found a place called Hedonism. I knew nothing about this resort, nor did I know what the definition of hedonism was, and Jack did not tell me anything. Hedonism was the only resort that was reasonably priced and would take us without a credit card. The resort was average but beautiful at the same time. The weather was beautiful, and the beach was remarkably close. The motel had been far from the beachfront, so this was a treat. I put on my bathing suit and went with Jack for a tour. I then realized that bathing suits were optional. I was very shocked to say the least, I was already uncomfortable with this entire situation. I was still in shock from leaving Samuel. Public nudity was not something that I was interested in. I am not a show-off when it comes to my body.

We ended up at the farthest sister resort that we were allowed to attend and there were naked people everywhere. If you were clothed you would feel uncomfortable because so many were not clothed. We went to the furthest hot tub and found people having sex. Jack was intrigued and wanted to take his clothes off. I reacted because I did not want to be the only one with clothes on. He very kindly put his clothes back on and needless to say we did not stay at that beach for long! I spent two weeks at the resort going back and forth to Jack's restaurant and bar. The entire journey was far from a relaxing experience; instead, it felt like I was inhabiting someone else's life. Nevertheless, it was also exhilarating, igniting the adventurous side of my personality and sending adrenaline coursing through my veins.

One night Jack took me dancing to the resort dance club. This was a treat because I spent most nights at his restaurant and bar sitting and waiting for him to be done. It was boring. I remember Jack looking so dapper in his fancy nightclub shirt and black pants. He was bold and brazen in appearance. I looked great as well. I had developed a tan and was losing more weight since I did not eat much due to the stress of leaving Samuel. When Jack was not working, we had fun together. He brought out the best in me. On the night of the dance things were different, however. He was on the phone, that was usual. I thought nothing of it. I was inside the dance club dancing and drinking while Jack was outside on the patio. I snuck up behind him to pinch his buttocks when I heard him say to the person on the phone, "I love you too baby, I miss you too."

My heart, which was already hurting from leaving Samuel and my doggie family behind, broke. As it turned out, Jack was living with a girl named Wanda. He tried to deny this but there was no denying it. The fact was when we first met, we both admitted to being in a relationship. Then, I moved away from Samuel and Jack told me that he had moved away from Wanda. But as usual he had lied. After that, I was finding out all sorts of information about Jack from his staff, including his night security guard. This man was a homeless, 20-something year old. Initially I thought that he did not like me. Then one day, after he knew that I had found out about Wanda, he approached me and said, "Finish this sentence, 'The Law of...?'". I looked at him in surprise and said, "Frickin' Attraction baby!" It was then that we became lifelong friends. His name was Moon, and so I called him Moon Baby. It fit for him and he loved it. We kept in touch after that for years.

The trip to Jamaica was an experience that I will always remember. I learned that Jack's friendship came at an expensive price. By the time I left the island, I was broke. Jack did not even come with me to the airport when I flew home. He sent me with his driver. It was not long after that we broke up. When I arrived back home, Maple was there to pick me up and she was happy to see me which surprised me. I knew she had not been happy that I had gone to Jamaica because she could see right through Jack.

Back in my hometown, I spent a number of days in a hotel to clear my mind. I heard through my family that Samuel was a mess, as I had expected. Nonetheless, there was nothing I could do to rectify the situation. We were over. I was supposed to stay at my eldest sister's place but it was too small for the both of us. When the money ran out from staying in hotels I went to stay at my friend Maple's place. My friend who had held my vehicle for me when I was in Jamaica gave into Samuel's demands and gave him my vehicle. I ended up renting one. Later that month I ran into friends at a car dealership where I went to look for a new vehicle. I had not seen them in awhile. They told me that they had a place for me to stay in their basement. Shortly afterwards I moved there. I was not accustomed to this way of living and I started to miss my former home. I was mourning that loss, the loss of my lifestyle, and all the comforts that came with it. Even though divorce does not result in the death of either party, one still goes through the mourning process. I certainly felt the repercussions of this. I also lost our joint friends. My parents took my leaving Samuel rather well. My siblings have remained friends with Samuel until this day, which I have mixed feelings about. I felt that Samual became closer to my siblings after I left.

Interestingly enough, after leaving Samuel, I stopped going to the casino as often. Later, I stopped going altogether. I was proud of myself. For the first time I felt that I could get my life together. I wanted to find my soulmate and live happily ever after. After coming back from Jamaica, I moved into a beautiful new condo. It was a new, 2-bedroom 2-bathroom suite in the nicest part of the city. I purchased all new furnishings and household items, and decorated it the way I wanted to. This was something that I was prohibited to do when I lived with Samual. It became my home sweet home. It was an oasis for me to heal from the changes and trauma that had occurred in my life.

Chapter Five- The Domino Effect

It wasn't long after I arrived back from Jamaica that my mother became ill. I remember very clearly the day she became critically ill. She ended up in the hospital, and I was in denial as to how ill she was. I stopped going to see her because I was afraid. I was afraid that she was dying, and she was. I did not know how to deal with that, so I tried to ignore it the best I could. During this time, my friend Joyce introduced me to a new group of psychics and mediums. These people were from a spiritual church in Alberta. I had arranged to go to one medium, named Samantha. My reading with her took place on Monday, April 29th, 2013, at 4 pm. I remember this reading like it was yesterday. Samantha told me that my mother's parents (my Grandparents) were there to "collect my mother." I had never met my Grandparents because they had died when my mother was only 13 years old. However, I had seen pictures of them. When they appeared to Samantha, I saw them. There was another message that "Spirit was there for me, giving me time to do whatever it was that I needed to do or say to my mother before she passed."

The very next day, I cleared my schedule and went to see my mother. I spent the day with her. She died that night at 9:45 pm. I was with her to watch her take her last breath. It was a haunting feeling that I had never had. I felt the spirit, I saw a spirit, and I sensed spirit with all my senses. My mother, for the first time in her life, was at peace. I am grateful for having been able to spend that time with her. Until this day, it sends shivers down my spine to think that the great Spirit and our loved ones arrive to collect us when we go to the nonphysical. I am truly a believer in Spirit, especially after this event. It changed my life forever and led me to a spiritual way of life. It was the beginning of a fascinating spiritual journey.

My mom's passing was one of the most challenging moments I have ever been through in my life. Helping my mom cross over was one of the purest moments in my life. I will never forget that time. It is mixed with emotions of gratitude, majestic moments of Spirit, and of loneliness. I knew my mom's spirit was around me through all my clair senses. I could feel her, see her and hear her. My sense of my mom's spirit grew even more intensely until one night when I was meditating. At that moment, my mom's spirit entered my body, and I felt my right eye go blind. My mother had been blind in her right eye. It was Spirit's way of telling me she was there, with me in spirit.

It amazes me to this day as to how real it felt when my mother's spirit came through to visit me. I believe that the right-eye blindness is my mother's signature, so that I can be aware of her presence. I always know when she's around when I feel my right eye go blind. It was an awakening of Spirit for me. As I have evolved spiritually, my mother has come through so strongly that she seems real to me. I can feel her presence, her breath, her soul. Her spirit is the strongest out of any spirit that I have felt. My mother's death was a pivotal time in my life. It was this moment that changed my life forever. It is the reason I strive to be the best medium and psychic I can be, to help others on their spiritual path. Spirit plays an essential role in our lives.

I remember organizing my mother's funeral. That was a terrifying time for me. I noticed a sudden shift in the family dynamics after my mother died. I felt all alone in the world after her passing. A piece of my heart was taken from me when my mother died that night. I remember going to the funeral home and going through all the details. The funeral home was very accommodating. We made a video for my mother's celebration of life. It showcased her life and what she was all about. I remember planning a celebration of life for my mom and my family left it up to me to plan the entire event. Jack had moved away, and I no longer had his support. Moms are incredibly special, as they are the ones who give birth to us. My mother and I were close. Because of this, I have come to appreciate mothers on an entirely different level. They are a pure gift from Spirit.

My mother was special to me. She believed in me. I miss having someone who loves me wholeheartedly, someone who has my back. It is something everyone should have in life. When this goes away, it is difficult to get it again. Most people have someone they can call who will take care of them if needed. I do not have anyone like that in my life. My mother's death came at the worst time in my life. Everything was happening at the same time. A month after my mother died, my two dogs died, a week apart from each other. This took its toll on me. For me, it was just as difficult getting over my two dogs' deaths as with any other death. Having my dogs die so closely after my mother was too much to handle; I crashed.

My mothers death was difficult on me because I never truly understood how much she meant to me until she was gone. She was my connection to the family until it started to slip away from me. I started to date two men at the same time. One of those was Hubert from Cameroon, Africa. He helped me through my mother's death and this helped me cope. The other boyfriend was Robert. I could not decide which boyfriend to date. I believe this was also due to mania. Weeks after my mother died, I was going to a spiritual church to a mediumship platform event where the resident mediums give the audience members messages. One message was for me. The message was from my mother and from both of my Babas (Ukrainian for grandmother). The message was clear and straightforward. It stated that what I was working on was not good for me, and I needed to make a change for the better. The message went on to say that neither of the boyfriends I had were right for me.

I was so angry. I remember being so attached to Hubert, but I was so unbalanced after my mother died that I could not cope very well. It was that night that I heard from my oldest sister that my two dogs had died. Hubert broke up with me that night also. I found out later that he was married and was expecting a baby. It was chaotic. I also found out at that time that Robert was dating someone else at the same time he was dating me. It was all too much to bear. I ingested a package of 12 allergy pills in the hopes of ending my life. There was no thought process with this. You eventually snap when things go haywire. You decide to end your life. I remember waking up the next morning feeling like crap. My stomach was hurting, and I had a reaction which was not good as a result of taking so many pills. I managed to survive this torture that I had put myself through.

Nonetheless, life sent me still more stress. A month after my dogs died, my good friend and co-worker Laureen died. She was my go-to girl when I needed someone to help me at work. She was the same age as I was. She had left my company and had started her own business. I had been so proud of her. It was so unexpected, that when I heard about her death, it sent shockwaves through me. It was too much grief and change all at once. I had found spirituality after my mother died, and it helped me through this terrible time. I did not fully understand then how terrible a time it was. My once familiar life had all but disappeared.

I had taken care of my parents for most of their senior life. Now, I was no longer capable of taking care of anyone else. My oldest sister's health was failing, and I was asked by my family to move in with her so that I could take care of her. I had to decline. As a result, I opted out of family life for that Christmas season of 2013. I scheduled a three-week cruise to the Caribbean islands. I would be gone for Christmas and New Year's. I needed to feed my destination addiction. I went by myself, something that I highly recommend. I had the time of my life. I missed my family, but since my mother died, I also felt like I was an orphan. I felt lonely and like I did not belong. The cruise was exactly what I needed at that time. I met so many people who helped me on my soul journey. I went swimming with the dolphins and snorkeling in the ocean. I danced and drank champagne at New Year's with friends who I had just met. It was the beginning of an exciting journey, and I felt my mother's spirit with me for the entire journey. The vacation to the Caribbean proved to be amazing. My father was well taken care of by my siblings, so I had no worries about leaving him behind and he had no worries about me. I felt that it was his time to spend with his children by himself now that his wife/my mother had passed on.

I came back home reluctantly from my vacation and found out that Joyce had booked us a trip to Mexico. Joyce and I then went on a 2-week vacation, where we saw the Law of Attraction guru Abraham Hicks. It was an amazing time. It helped further my addiction to Spirit and the Law of Attraction. It truly fed my soul. Joyce ended up buying a timeshare and one of the perks was a trip to the Dominican Republic. So shortly after the trip to Mexico, Joyce and I trotted off again on an adventure to the Dominican Republic. We had the time of our lives as Joyce and I had our very own pool in the backyard of the condo. During this vacation I met a lovely 20-something man named Leo. He was studying to be a lawyer. We hit it off and went on a few dates while I was there. It was a time I would not forget. I remember leaving for the airport to return home; I started to cry uncontrollably. I understand now that I had been manic on that trip. Joyce knew that something was not right, but we did not address the issue at that time.

When we arrived back home to Canada, Spirit was grabbing hold of me, and I was fighting for a new life. To alleviate the grief from my mother's death, Joyce counseled me with EFT, the Emotional Freedom Technique, otherwise known as tapping. As a therapist, Joyce sat down with me and we discussed how I was feeling. We would tap on the meridian points. As we continued to tap, we would discuss my feelings and where these feelings stemmed from. We kept on tapping until I no longer had an emotional attachment to that issue. As Joyce and I tapped, we came to the point where we discussed my father's mother, my Baba Mary. Mary did not love me the way she did the other grandchildren. In Mary's eyes, I was the other woman's child.

As we continued to dig deeper, we started to address my allergies and where they stemmed from. As a young child, I had always been extremely allergic to feathers. As we continued to tap, what came out was astonishing to me. The image that came to me was one of torture. I was five years old when my Baba Mary and Grandpa John were slaughtering chickens. They were doing this in the barn, and my father walked me into this dark, dingy place. I then saw my Baba Mary pick up a live chicken and put it on the table and chop its head off. She then let it loose to run around the yard until it died. With me being an empath, this was horrible to watch. I felt sick to my stomach, and I was terrified. This was something that I never forgot. It was then that I developed allergies to feathers, feather pillows, feather quilts, and so on. We tapped this away and after that, I did not have a problem with feathers. It was amazing to find out that tapping worked. It released an emotional blockage that I did not know was there until the counseling session.

Regarding my rape however, I blocked this from myself so I could not feel my emotions. I never wanted to discuss how being raped really made me feel. Deep inside I felt powerless, weak, and betrayed. However, if you don't release past emotions, they will come back as ailments, disorders, and diseases as they did with me. Spirit and tapping helped me with my relationship with my Baba Mary long after she had passed. I have had closure with our relationship and have forgiven her for making me feel left out. Baba Mary's spirit has arrived several times during mediumship readings after these tapping sessions, and as a result, that part of my life has been healed. What I can now understand is that I started to develop more allergies after I was raped. I did not tap on this with Joyce. I did not release these emotions or allergies from my energy body. They were still buried inside of my virtual Pandora's box.

The lingering sorrow I was feeling ran deeply, escaping my awareness. I was oblivious to the emotions that I had because I had buried them deep inside. This would set off a domino effect. Being an empath, my vibration has been filled with negative emotions my entire life. These emotions and negative vibrations have left me powerless. I have had a lot of changes in my life. Some of us can recover from change more easily than others, depending on how much change has occurred. Another factor is how much support is around you to help you recover from a challenging situation. I can tell you firsthand that having bipolar does not help when you are going through change. Change is something that has made me unstable.

After all the destruction and loss in my life, I met a new friend named Kazey, and we became close. He helped me through this time. He was from Rwanda, Africa. This is where the genocide occurred. He lost eight family members in the war, who were slaughtered in front of him with machetes. He spent three months hiding in rice fields. He shared this with me when I, too, was grieving. Kazey's story helped to change my life to a more spiritual one. It helped put things into perspective about our soul journeys and how everyone has their own story to tell. It made me realize that life is too short to be unhappy. Kazey and I started to date. It was during this time however that I was sexually assaulted by a friend of his. I was staying at Kazey's place when he went to the store, and I fell asleep in his bed. His friend came in and sexually assaulted me. I screamed, and he ran away. I brushed this off as just a mishap. Kazey and I broke up right afterwards. The person who sexually assaulted me died in a fight shortly after. This was a terrible time for me, and the feeling of this man groping me when I half asleep was horrifying. It made me more emotionally unstable. My emotional health was starting to crash, and I did not realize it.

What I did to distract myself was to engross myself in Spirit. I did this to take my mind off things, much like I did before when I was raped.

However this time was different, I was older and was starting to do spiritual/ soul growth to deepen my connection to spirit. Little did I know that this spiritual enlightenment would open up my Pandora's box. In my turmoil, I stopped using tapping to release my emotions. I forgot how well it worked until later in my journey. All I knew was that I was grieving the loss of my home, and of family and friends who had passed. Living unknowingly with bipolar, it was the beginning of a soon-to-be life crisis. I realized that life was too sacred, and that Spirit was calling. I had been searching for answers as to why people pass on the way they do. Spirit answered my call. I started to attend spiritual classes as well as mediumship and tarot courses with Samantha. I became a Reiki practitioner, as well as taking courses on numerology and other mystic Arts. This type of mysticism fed my soul. This was something that I needed.

I found solstice in the local spiritual church where the classes were held. I felt like I belonged there. Later, Samantha introduced me to a church on Vancouver Island, Canada that they were affiliated with. Harry was a renowned medium there. Mediumship students from all over would attend to learn the mystic art of mediumship. I was scheduled to attend several courses with Harry during the year of 2014-2015. When I first met Harry, it was a haunting feeling, as if his spirit touched mine. I felt his power from God run through my soul and touch my heart on a deep level. Maybe it was the fact that I first saw him at the altar of the church as I sat in the audience. It was a spiritual feeling indeed. What I can understand now is that he felt safe. I felt Spirit nearby. I know that I found the Great Spirit when I first met Harry. The words he preached touched my soul.

I was chosen to be in Harry's class in the mediumship course that summer. I was excited. In the course we were not allowed to use our cell phones. They wanted the experience to be truly spiritual, and I agreed. I did not use my phone for seven days, the entire duration of the class. The course proved to be just what I was looking for to advance my mediumship skills. I thought the people were lovely that I met at this course. I did not want this course to end as I loved it so much. At the end of this course, I was scheduled to go back home to Alberta. The next day as I prepared to leave for the airport, I did a quick five-minute meditation. During this meditation, I saw a crisp, clear, vision of Harry in my mind's eye. This vision haunted me because it was as if he were alive inside my mind. I wasn't sure why I was being shown my teacher/minister's face, but it was eerie.

On my trip back to Alberta, I had a two-hour layover in Vancouver. I had dinner there, and the restaurant sold glasses of champagne. I felt that this was a sign from Spirit. The entire day was filled with serendipitous moments, or what I call signs from Spirit. There was a mystical feeling in the air that day. The luggage cart on the runway had my birth year on it, and the flight had the numbers of my birth date. I felt that the signs were significant. I knew something was about to happen in my life but wasn't sure what it would be. I felt Spirit everywhere, and my psychic senses were activated.

As I started to sip my glass of champagne in the Vancouver airport, I reluctantly turned my cell phone on, and as I did, I received a phone call from my oldest sister. She was calling to tell me that our father had died that day in the morning. It was Father's Day Sunday. As we talked, she told me the time he died. It was the same time that I saw Harry's face, another sign from Spirit. It was heartbreaking news to hear, and Father's Day will never be the same for me. Looking back, I realized that my mother's spirit had come to me that day as well in a dream. It was a haunting feeling, but I had brushed it off as nothing. As it turned out, my father became ill that week while I was away, and he died shortly after. My sister told me he was diagnosed with colon cancer, and when he heard the news, he told the nurse he wanted to die. He did just that. He passed away to the Great Spirit. The event of my Father's death helped fuel the onset of mania for me. I did not realize it then. I realized that losing my father on Father's Day hit me harder than I had previously thought. The absence of both my parents in my life left a substantial void in my sense of self. Becoming an adult orphan was one of the hardest life transitions that I have experienced.

Just after I got off the phone with my sister, Jack called telling me he was in town. Jack and I had remained friends after we broke up because we were kindred spirits. We were drawn to each other. I told him about my loss and he consoled me. When I arrived home, I felt different, empty inside from the pain of losing my father. That night my father's spirit came to me. I heard him say to me, "I can hear again." In life my father had terrible hearing. When I heard that, it made me believe even more in Spirit. I will never forget that day. My father sounded happy, like he was set free from the pain that life had brought. It made my soul connect to my spirit on a deep level. Later that week, Jack and I went out to one of our favorite pubs and drank champagne to celebrate my father's life. Jack helped me with my grief. He helped me find some sort of peace with all that was happening.

Just before I left for my mediumship course, I had had the idea to interview my father with the voice recorder on my phone, about his life, his children, and his thoughts. It took a few hours of my time and what was created was a beautiful memory that we now have of our father. My sister compiled the voice recordings and combined it in a video, so his voice is playing with photographs of his life. It is a beautiful legacy of my father that we have to look back on. My siblings and I cleaned up the affairs of my father. We had his celebration of life a month later. All my family attended. It was an incredibly sad time. What I can understand now is that my father's passing was a pivotal moment that lead me to mentally crash.

During this time, I remember feeling so heavy both spiritually and physically. I used food as a coping mechanism. As a result of my stress, my thyroid became low, and I lost a lot of my hair. I had no energy, and I could barely keep active. I took natural medicine to remedy this, but it took time to heal. I felt suicidal but told no one. Little did I know suicidal tendencies are a risk in bipolar disorder. What saved me was Spirit. I found Spirit in a more profound sense during this time. Spirit helped pull me up and give me the life that I needed.

It was then that bipolar disorder became activated in my life so strongly that I could not ignore it. I was unaware and untreated. I reacted in ways that were not balanced, and I took little notice of the repercussions of my behaviors. Darkness climbed inside my soul and held me captive. I started to be consumed with grief, pain, and sorrow. I believe that is why so many people with mental illness throughout the world commit suicide and are successful at it. They go through life without treatment.

As the months went by, I decided to take an Alaskan cruise. I was planning to take some of my father's ashes and spread them in the ocean near Alaska. The cruise was in September of 2015. My father had taken us to Alaska as children, so this place carried fond memories for me. On a cruise ship excursion, I went salmon fishing to honor my father. He was an amazing fisherman. I remember spreading my father's ashes in the ocean when I was on the fishing boat. As I spread his ashes in the ocean, I felt my father's spirit come alive, and then a bald eagle swept by my head. The fishing boat captain was surprised and said that this never happens so close to someone. I then knew it was confirmation that it was my father's spirit. It was then that I acknowledged the eagle to be my spirit animal.

Soon after, Joyce developed cancer and passed away. The death of my parents and my friend Joyce sent shockwaves through me as they were the people who actually knew me on a soul level.

Chapter Six- The Island of Hope

During this turbulent time, I did my best to keep positive, but it was difficult. I felt like I was unable to keep up with life's changes. Once more, I pushed my emotions aside and concealed them in Pandora's box, unaware of the deeper, hidden emotions yet to be unveiled. I tried to rebuild my life through Spirit on a deeper level. I started to attend church to lead a more spiritual life than I had before. I had big plans to expand my business to a nationwide franchise. I had a business partner lined up, and I participated in interviews for the television show, "The Dragons Den", a television show about business development. For the first time in my life, I felt that I could conquer this grief and turmoil. I was then nominated for the Woman's Entrepreneur Award and the Woman of Vision Business Award. It was a peak in my career. I felt that my old life was over, and that I was starting again. My soul was calling, and I felt for the first time in my life that I was starting to heal. I was going back and forth From Alberta to British Columbia to take mediumship studies with Harry. I did this a few times a year, and when I was in Alberta, I studied with Samantha and Steve, who were teachers and spiritual ministers.

I decided that I needed to change my life, so I poured myself into personal development. I started to work out with a personal trainer, and I lost weight. When I had first met Jack, I was very heavy. For the first time in my life, I knew that I could conquer my weight issue. However, regarding my emotions, I was so used to the emotional roller coaster that bipolar puts you on that I became used to it. I pushed the emotions aside and strived to start a new life.

I engrossed myself in spiritual teachings, the Law of Attraction, as well as in the teachings of Abraham Hicks. One of her teachings states that one should stay away from any negativity for 30 days. I did this. I had as little association with people as possible—no television, no news, nothing that would alter my vibration to the negative in the slightest, only positivity. I did this with such success, it changed my life and gave me a reason to live again. I started a dream/ vision board so that I could manifest my desires. I came out of my slump. I even started to eat healthier. I listened only to Abraham's teachings. I did this all day, every day. Thirty days turned into sixty days. This changed my focus from grieving victim to empowered superwoman.

After my 30-day challenge, my mediumship was on fire. I found comfort in my mediumship studies. No one mentioned to me that doing mediumship when you are in trauma and grieving is not recommended. I engrossed myself in mediumship. I loved it. That is when I found spirituality on a deeper level. It saved me and gave me a new lease on life. I started to train to become a platform medium. This is when you step on stage in an auditorium and give messages to people in the audience who are wishing to hear from their loved ones who have passed. It was a different way of life for me and something that I craved. It felt like it fit 100% for me.

I was training to become a platform evidential spiritual medium. I was channelling loved ones who had crossed over to Spirit. I provided bits of spiritual evidence that I channeled from spirit which only the loved one could understand. This was to give them hope that it was genuinely their loved one coming through. This is the light of faith which I call Spirit. I believe that Spirit is all around us, and it is here guiding us to a more peaceful life. Its role is to help us on our journey and communicate with us that life is eternal. It is a simple message stating that all is well.

I was busy all of the time, so I did not have time to think. I did all of this while successfully running my beauty empire which consisted of 16 beauty salons. I had a lot on my plate and added more as time went on. I felt that mediumship gave me balance from work. It was my pleasure. During one reading, I was getting a song playing in my mind by Johnny Horton. It was the focus of my thoughts. I heard the song, and so I stepped on stage with this tidbit of information for the audience, hoping that it was not my thoughts playing tricks on me. Suddenly, a person put up their hand and said that this message was for them. Their father played in the Johnny Horton Band. I went on to finish the message, and it was all correct. That was my first mediumship message experience on the stage. It proved to be very exhilarating, knowing that I can help others find peace as it did with me when I had received messages.

The next message was for a lady in the audience. It was her grandmother who had passed. I gave all my evidence, what her grandmother did for work and how she had lived her life. I described her in detail and went on and on with profound evidence for the client. She would not take any of this information in until I mentioned the word suicide. It was then the lady took in the information. Once I mentioned suicide, she took all the information and went on to explain what had happened. It made me happy as it helped to heal this lady. The lady thanked me for the message that I had given her. I became remarkably close to this spiritual community in Alberta. They helped me grow and develop my skills while at the same time, gave me comfort during this troubled time.

We had a spiritual meetup we called a "circle." Thus, I named this group of mediums my Circle Soul Sisters. A circle is when a committed group of people sit together regularly on the same day, time, and location, to build and work with Spirit. They were a group of people who were helping me evolve spiritually in my journey of life. In this circle we became the closest of friends. This circle made my heart sing. I was eager to get more out of life. For the first time in my life, I found that I was a free woman. I was an orphan, with nothing to tie me down. I felt the urge to go see Samantha for another mediumship reading. During this reading, Spirit stated to me that if I wanted to change my life that Spirit would not help me with that. I had to do it on my own. If I wanted a different life, it was up to me to make a move. It was then that I decided to make a spontaneous move to Vancouver Island, British Columbia. By the end of that day, I had it all planned out, as brief as that plan was.

I took the reading from Samantha, looked at the vision board that I had created with the picture of the ocean, and decided to move. I gave notice to leave my beautiful condo in February of 2016. I would move in with my friend Maple for a few months to save money, so that I could afford to move to the new province. This decision saved me from paying my $1550 per month condo rent. I would sell everything I owned, all the new furnishings, household items, decorations and mementos that I had very carefully picked out for my little oasis.

I was oblivious to the fact that my bipolar disorder had already consumed my life. After that, I spent no time at all planning. I did not think to contact my connections at the church on the Island to let them know that I was coming to stay. I was flying by the seat of my pants. I was scheduled to attend another mediumship course with Harry for June that year, 2016. I set the plan in action to move into a place in July 2016. I listened to what Spirit was telling me. I sold all my belongings and gave my oldest sister my state-of- the-art new 65-inch television. I sold all the other items that I had just purchased. It was a scary yet exciting time.

I did not realize the stress involved in moving and what exactly it entailed until later. I found out through research that there is such as thing as transitional trauma, where you go through the loss of the former place you lived. I was not prepared for this. I was not prepared to move at all. All I thought about was Spirit and my mediumship studies. Transitional trauma can appear in people of any age undergoing change, particularly when it's abrupt. Symptoms include depression and anxiety. The bottom line is that any type of change can bring on unwanted stress. However, due to my bipolar disorder, my emotions often swung to extremes, and during periods of happiness, I experienced a natural high.

Most of the time, my vibration was in alignment with the Great Spirit. I was on the high-flying disk that Abraham states is a great place to be when your vibration is high, and you are centered within yourself. Nothing seemed to bother me. I would get signs from Spirit daily which led me to believe that I was on the right path. There were signs like 11:11 on the clock or a feather falling from the sky. My mother would come through from Spirit to give me comfort through signs, such as the theme from the old television show "The Littlest Hobo" playing in my mind. This was my mother giving me this memory. It was as if her spirit were with me on this journey, rooting for me and laughing with me. I was like that hobo in the television show, but I was laughing at myself too. I felt elated one moment and in utter despair the next. I pressed on.

You never really know where life will take you. I left with only what could fit in my leased Ford Explorer. I named my vehicle Walter—this was my father's middle name. Walter and I set off on a journey with my traveling partner Sheila. Sheila was a friend who I had met after I gave her a psychic reading. I agreed to pay for Sheila's flight home if she would travel with me, so I would not have to be alone. I was elated with the thought of going to the new province. There was no thought process of where, or how I was going to live. I followed my soul and went to this island of hope. I was unprepared for what I would find. I did not do any research on how I would find a doctor or a place to live. I did not research the demographics and geography. I just prayed to Great Spirit, and it led the way. All I knew was that I had less than one week to find a place. Then I would be attending the mediumship course for seven days. The course was scheduled for the week of June 13th, 2016. I would have a place to stay during this time, as they provided the accommodations during the course. After that, I would be homeless. Actually, I was homeless after leaving my condo, which is a scary thought looking back now.

The journey to the island was seamless, with no worries at all. I was so happy that I did not think about anything from the past that would worry or hurt me. I remember arriving in Vancouver and going into the line up for the ferry. I started to have a meltdown. I wasn't sure why except for the thought ran across my mind that I was officially going to live on an island, and to get off, you would need to fly out or catch the ferry. That thought was scary to me. I arrived on Vancouver Island and stayed at the motel, a small 1960's retro-styled motel. I had stayed there before to attend Harry's weekend mediumship retreats and soul classes. I knew the lady who ran the motel well.

My friend Sheila and I went for walks and went out on the town. The first place we went to was a beautiful pub overlooking the Inner Harbour. We had a stunning ocean view from our table. We had drinks and met a nice fellow named Jamie. As Jamie and I spoke, we immediately hit it off. Jamie worked for a coupon book organization. I told him that I was interested in getting a part-time job to keep me busy. I wanted to meet people and thought this would give me what I needed—some new friends and a purpose in life. Jamie said he was looking for someone on a part-time basis to help him distribute his coupon books. I agreed and had a job! Things were looking up. They were certainly in alignment with what I wanted.

The next day I arranged to view four places to rent. I decided to contact the church to see if they knew of any place. I contacted the church and spoke to the minister, Tanis, and asked if she knew anyone who would be looking to rent a room. She said that she had a room to rent until October and the rent was only $300 per month. This was a steal as I was used to paying $1550 per month for my condo. Tanis and I agreed that I would rent her room sight unseen. I canceled my other bookings, and during the time that I had left with Sheila, we enjoyed touring around. It was a time that I will never forget. I had a new job, a place to live, and everything was going in the right direction. I had hired a new manager, Gertrude, to help me run my salons back in Alberta. As the days came and went, it was soon time for Sheila to head back to Alberta.

The very next day, my Circle Soul Sisters Jane and Dana were coming for the course from Alberta, so I was able to enjoy a day with them before we headed to the retreat center where our week-long mediumship retreat was to be held. It was then that things started to turn bumpy. On the way to the retreat center, Gertrude phoned to tell me that one of our salons was canceling our lease. This was due to the conduct of one of the hairdressers. They would not give us another chance. I tried not to let it bother me, but it did. Knowing that I was not going to be using my phone and that I would not be reachable during the course, sent my alignment out of whack. My emotions fluctuated due to bipolar disorder, experiencing highs and lows.

I went to the course with Jane and Dana. As the course started, everyone was gifted with a beautiful eagle pendant. Just before I opened the box to look inside, I heard a message from Spirit stating, "This is from Harry." The eagle was my spirit animal. Spirit animals, also called spirit guides and power animals, come in and out of our lives depending on the direction that we are going and the tasks we need to complete along our journey. They are here to guide us. I would often get signs like this from Spirit having to do with Harry. I brushed this idea of the spirit animal off and went to join the rest of the group. It was then that I saw Minister Tanis. She would also be at the course because she was one of the assistants. Minister Tanis told me that Harry had picked out the pendants this time. She went on to say that usually this was her job but this time Harry decided to pick something. This was another sign, I thought to myself.

A few days into the course, Minister Tanis pulled me aside and told me that I would not be a good fit to move into her place. So there I was on an island and homeless. Not only did it send me out of alignment, but it also accelerated my mania. I did not know what bipolar was at the time, nor did I understand that I was manic. However, looking back, I can see now that I was. I did not let the situation get me down. In the course, we meditated for one hour in the morning and one hour in the evening, so it was easy to get back into alignment when I was centering myself. Thank heavens for meditation. It does help to clear the mind and give one a fresh perspective. However, meditation does not get rid of bipolar or mania—medication is required for that.

I had concerns regarding my mediumship and spiritual studies. In Alberta, I was going to the church to do my mediumship studies and to spiritual circles three days per week. I was committed to my craft. However, I had rarely gone to the Sunday service in Alberta. Church service was not something that I was accustomed to growing up. As an adult, it was not something that I thought about. However, Spirit had been calling me my entire life. Spirit would always put me in direct alignment with churches and spirits to help guide me. It was something that I never acted on. Spirit was giving me a strong call to action to attend the church on Sunday in my new city.

Going to the Sunday service at the spiritual church where Harry was minister, would give me an outing and something to do. I asked to speak to Harry privately. I wanted to ask him about the weekly mediumship training that they offered through their church. I had heard that it was typically booked up for years, and you had to be asked to join. I wanted to ask him about this and what I should do for training as I was used to training three days or more per week. The days passed and Harry finally had time to come and see me. We sat across from each other and spoke about what I should do. The conversation was short and sweet. He asked how I planned to support myself and stated that the economy in British Columbia was not the same as in Alberta, as Alberta was booming at that time. I smiled and told him that I had 16 beauty salons running in Alberta. He seemed surprised and said not to worry about the weekly course but to just get through the summer first.

This was not exactly what I was looking for, but I took it all in stride. I do, however, remember my bipolar moments during the course. I would go to my room and cry when I could. I kept a brave face otherwise and did my best to forget the difficult moments. The bipolar lows were so low during this course that I thought of dying. In class, Harry looked at me as he addressed the class and asked why anyone would want to die. It was as if he were speaking directly to me, and as if he were reading my mind. I had told no one of my emotions. Unaddressed bipolar is like you are a walking time bomb waiting to go off. I wish I had known I was off kilter back then. If I had addressed my emotions at the time, it would have changed my life. I had become accustomed to the emotional roller coaster that bipolar put me through. What I did to get my focus off my emotions was to dive deep into my spiritual studies.

I had already taken my turn at platform mediumship where we get on stage in front of everyone and give a message from Spirit to someone in the audience. It was our class, and Harry was our teacher, guiding us, and he would often get the same spirit, so he was able to tell you if you were right or not. I felt safe that I would not have to get up again to do another reading because with the class size we would often only have one chance to do it. This time was different. Near the end of the class, Harry called me up to do a platform reading. I reluctantly obliged, and sheepishly walked over to the stage. As I stood there, Harry's father came in from Spirit, and I knew that I had a message from Spirit for my teacher. I tried to pawn the spirit off on another lady, but it was not for her, and I knew it. I said to Harry, "I have your father." Harry simply said to me, "I know you do." I went on to give what was probably one of the best readings of my life. Months prior, I had prayed to Spirit, stating that if Harry was meant to be mine, to bring his father in for me in a reading. I don't know what made me pray for that because I had never really found Harry attractive physically. I was simply drawn to him spiritually and on a soul level. Harry's father appearing set the tone for a great rest of the course as I knew then that Spirit was on my side.

I tried not to think about killing myself but the lows of bipolar disorder hit me hard. The course ended, and I went to the motel. I planned to drink champagne. The champagne was off-limits during the mediumship course, so I now wanted to treat myself. My Circle "Soul" sister, Jane from Alberta, was leaving the following day. We had arranged to spend the last night together in celebration. Before leaving for the evening, I checked my email. I had received a message from an advertisement that I had posted. I had stated that

I was looking for a place to rent. No one had replied previously, so I had forgotten about the advertisement. I replied to the message. It turned out to be a beautiful two-bedroom, one-bathroom, bottom-level suite in a house, available July 1st. It was in one of the nicest neighborhoods on the island and it was located two blocks from the ocean! Jane and Dana checked the place out with me, and I immediately took it.

I arranged to stay a few nights with friends who I had met at the course. Martin and his wife Mandy, and Mildred. It would help me build bonds with the locals. I could also save money on renting the room at the motel. I started to get excited about moving into my new place. I planned on sleeping on the floor until I could manage to get furniture. Everything was working out and flowing seamlessly. It was all in divine timing. I was in alignment with what I wanted. As it turned out, the lady who had previously lived in the 2-bedroom suite was giving away her queen size bed. She offered it to me and I gratefully accepted. There were these types of synchronicities along my journey.

Chapter Seven- Spirit's Whispers

I had arrived in this oceanfront city with a new sense of myself. Although I felt footloose and fancy free one moment, I felt in utter despair in the next. The spiritual community that I knew well from numerous mediumship and soul courses helped me from getting out of balance. This new experience was a delight, and I was fighting hard to start a new life. I thought I was in alignment with that which I wanted. I attended the church and went to events such as the July 1st church party. I went with a new friend who I met at a few of the courses I took at the church. Her name was Hilda and she was looking to move to the Island as well. She was also in the process of getting a divorce. We became instant friends, and we started to hang out together regularly, which was nice or so I thought. We also attended church together.

Hilda was very eager to get into the popular group in the church, so she started that process by asking for a meeting with Minister Tanis. I was not fond of Tanis after she did not allow me to live at her place. I understand now that I was too outgoing for Tanis. I brushed the idea of getting in with the popular group aside. However, I remembered a reading that Mildred had given me when I stayed at her place. In the reading, Spirit said that I was to go as often as possible to the church. So I did, and I always kept that in mind if there was another gathering taking place.

I also met a lovely friend named Bill. He was married and loved mediumship and the church. He went often, and we became friends. He would tour me around town showing me the sights. I would also see Martin and Mandy often, and I was working part-time with Jamie. I was building my life once again, and everything was in order. I managed to sell two of my largest salons, and that gave me some extra money to buy the rest of my furniture. That summer was filled with sun, fun, and ocean—everything that I loved. I found peace and spirituality through Harry's community. It changed my life for the better. The church gave me balance and stability. Church time was peaceful and it provided structure. It kept me distracted from thinking of everything that I had left behind and of not understanding the emotional roller coaster that I was on.

My sisters came to see me for a week, and I drove them around, showing them my new city. Our visit was a time I will never forget as it strengthened our bond as a family. This was much needed, and I felt loved. That first summer on Vancouver Island was a dream. One day, I looked in the mirror, thinking that I should get a haircut when I heard a voice stating to me that I should grow it long. I thought it was Spirit telling me this. I was feeling Spirit even stronger than before, and I would get messages like this daily. I was in alignment. As Abraham Hicks states, I was on my "high-flying disc", meaning that I was connected.

My other Circle Soul Sister, Brandi, was coming to visit from Alberta. She too was planning to move to Vancouver Island. She came to stay with me so that she could pick out a condo to purchase. She was a medium, just like me. One night we were having some drinks, and I was telling Brandi that Spirit was communicating with me. I mentioned the message of not cutting my hair, and she told me that she thought it was Harry, and not Spirit telling me that. Brandi stated that Harry had been a medium his entire life and had been trained at a young age. He was capable of much more than one might think, she said. She thought it was him who was communicating with me via telepathy. This gave me something to think about. I told my friend Hilda about this, and she informed me that she would get messages from Harry during meditation. That gave me such a realization. Hilda went on to tell me that she had a secret crush on one of the other male minsters at Harry's church and that she thought that she was in love. This entire situation baffled me and made me think of Spirit on a completely different level.

I felt that it was Spirit and not Harry who was communicating with me. I felt Spirit was a guide showing me the way to the light. However, Brandi told me that Harry was one of the best mediums around and that if anybody could communicate through telepathy, it was him. This brought me back to one reading that I had had with Samantha. In that reading, Spirit was telling me that I would be meeting a teacher who I would become close to, and that this teacher would change my life. This message now intrigued me. It made me think of the time that I saw a vision of Harry when my father died. Had Harry been brought into my life because my father passed, a concept in which some people of First Nation descent believed? It made me think of all those psychic readings in which I had been told that I would meet a teacher who would change my life. Nonetheless, I felt uncertain about the life-changing aspect of the reading.

My feelings toward Harry were not romantic. They were spiritual, and I had not experienced anything like it before. It was something that baffled me. The funny thing was we had only spoken a few words to each other. Our relationship was strictly professional. So why were we spiritually connected? To this day I have no answers. But I know that we were connected spiritually to learn from each other. At that time I was yet to understand this. My telepathy experience with Harry is one of my Pandora's box of secrets which I share with you. It was a secret which started to consume me. It gave me something to be happy about. I started to think about Harry often and would look forward to seeing him at the church. I was, however, professional around him and did not give him the idea that I liked him in a personal sort of way. The day of the church session became the highlight of my week, although I would only see Harry on stage.

I started to feel like my life was perfect. I felt like I was just starting to get things back together. I had it all, including a beautiful home in one of the nicest neighborhoods with all new furnishings. I had a high income to provide me with a charming, comfortable lifestyle. My business was earning over 350K per year. Gambling was now a thing of the past, and I was able to communicate with Spirit. Everything was going great. However, the fact that I had this mystery to solve regarding my connection to Harry baffled me. I did not tell anyone about these coincidences other than Brandi, Hilda, Martin, and Mandy. No one had answers for me. I went on to enjoy the summer attending church and it became a beautiful time in my life. I attended church on Sundays, which took up most of the day, as there would be coffee and bagels after, which I always looked forward to.

Nonetheless, Sundays proved to be the most challenging day of the week for me. When my parents were alive, I spent every Sunday with them, rain or shine. It didn't matter how I was feeling or who I was dating. My parents had demanded my time on Sundays, and for the most part, I had enjoyed these visits. I realized that after they passed, there was a substantial void in my life. The Spiritual church became a much-needed distraction to help me get through my grieving process. I also decided that Sunday nights would be my movie and dinner night with champagne. I made it a weekly routine to treat myself to a nice dinner with drinks.

Thursday was the day I most looked forward to because it was meditation/ healing night at the Church. My newly acquired friends and I would go and receive spiritual healing at the front of the church. However, I did not choose to go up to the alter. I only took part in the meditation. To get the healing, one would need to go to the front of the church and sit in one of the chairs. The spiritual healers would stand behind the person and place their hands on the person's shoulders for a few minutes. Spirit would then go in and heal what needed to be healed. I was always too shy to go up there. The meditation would then start. It was a fantastic time for me. Harry would guide us through the meditation, and I would sit in the audience as he would gently guide us. My mind would float away with the Great Spirit—it was superb.

Spirituality gave me something to live for. It helped give me comfort after losing so much. It gave me something to look forward to. For the first time in my life, I felt like I belonged. I had met an entirely new demographic of friends. Spirituality became my entire life and helped me grow on a soul level. It put me in a more positive frame of mind. I started to attend church services, weekly circles, and classes on various subjects: Tarot, Healing, Reiki, Color Therapy, Spirituality, Meditation, Soul Exploration, Psychic Development, Spiritual Mediumship, and Numerology. I also attended workshops on other subjects in the spiritual world, such as Scrying, Tea Leaf reading, Psychometry, and Energy Psychology.

This group changed my life for the better and they felt like family to me. This spiritual community opened my universe. I met so many people from around the world during my spiritual mediumship classes. We were all like-minded, spiritual, and were a very close-knit society, even though we were scattered worldwide. I had spiritual friends in Switzerland, Canada, and all over the United States. Being in this spiritual community made me realize that I would love to inspire people through my spirituality one day. I have always wanted to inspire people with my story and to help them understand their own life as I have learned to understand mine. I realized that my goal was to become a motivational speaker and possibly even a spiritual minister in the Spiritual Church. I had a deep love for this community. It was healing me, so I wanted to share my journey with others. The only way I knew how to inspire people is through ministry. I was aware that ministers could help people in need, and that is what I wanted to do. I wanted to inspire people.

Additionally, I was starting to lose weight and I was feeling on top of the world. The manager of my salons in Alberta, Gertrude, quit, and as it turned out, she did not do any of the work that she had said she would do. As bad as that was, I kept in alignment, and I was on fire. I hired a personal assistant, and she helped me grow my business and get it ready to expand to British Columbia. We were working on a costly new accounting system—I would need to do that to streamline the processes. We had a plan, and it was working out perfectly. However, it was an expensive process to acquire, one that was necessary to my achieving success with this new venture.

When I wasn't planning my new empire, I attended spiritual events at the church. I felt so good that I registered to attend the healer's course in October. I had been told numerous times that I was a born healer. I remembered the times when I would see healing being done in such an overly dramatic way that it was unbelievable. On the other hand, what I was to learn was not the dramatized healing that you see in movies. This healing was beautiful, simple, and understated. I was told that the healing course was essential for a medium as it helps one's mediumship grow to new levels.

The church was going so well I registered to become an official member of the congregation and take a spiritual course through the Church. I also had pre-booked courses for the 2017 season for my mediumship under Harry's tutorial. I could sense that Hilda was jealous regarding this. She wanted to go to these courses but needed to save her money. I now understand that this put an obstacle in the way of our friendship. I remember my mediumship becoming so outstanding that it surprised me. I would sense spirit and people's vibrations on a deeper level. My emotions were becoming out of control—I was extremely high or exceptionally low—with no in-between. Being bipolar in general is one thing that I can handle. Being manic is quite another thing. I found the mania to be too much of a roller coaster. Think of the world's most colossal roller coaster, and each turn is a different emotion—that is mania. That is what it feels like to be in that world, like you are in this chaotic, supernova world full of magic.

Spirit's whispers consumed my mind, and I could tell the difference between Harry's telepathy and Spirit's whispers. By this time, Spirit was more evident to me than ever before. In the fall of 2016, the messages or thoughts became more evident. One night, I heard songs in my head from the '80s. I did not listen to 80's music during that time. It intrigued me enough to want to find out what the tune was. I would look up the song that was playing in my mind. It was indeed a song from the '80s. The very next day at Church, the theme was the 80's. This made my jaw drop. I tried to brush this off as Spirit, not as Harry. I said nothing to Harry. In confidence, I told Hilda, my medium friend from Church. She was convinced that it was Harry and was perplexed. Looking back, I should have told Harry, but I did not. I brushed this off as pure Spirit.

Other times also confused me like the time I went home from the Thursday evening meditation and healing at Church. Just as I arrived home, I had a thought that came across my mind, the word "chastity," and then I heard "look that up." So I did. Chastity is the state of not having sex with anyone or only having sex with your husband or wife. The thought did not come from me. It was coming from a spirit. I thought that it was perhaps Harry because I heard the word, Harry. I was a medium and was able to communicate with spirit discarnate (passed). It wasn't that far off to believe that I could hear messages from spirit incarnate (living). However, I was only a mediumship student, and I needed a medium teacher to sort out this spiritual mess. But I did not go to Harry until much later in my journey.

What made me believe that I was communicating with Harry through telepathy was the fact that when Harry teaches with other people, they do not talk much during the course. Some students believe that they are communicating through telepathy. So I started to believe this to be true for myself. That entire fall was filled with mystery and magic. I started to give psychic and mediumship readings on some clients. I worked with one client as a result of the reading with Harry's dad that day in class. One of my classmates approached me right after I gave Harry his reading and wanted me to give her daughter a reading. That was the first professional reading that I had done on the Island. The reading went well, and it gave me the confidence that I was on the right track spiritually and was very well connected to the source energy of the Great Spirit.

Chapter Eight- The Key to Pandora's Box

If I had ever believed in destiny, now would be the time because everything has spiritually led at this point to my true destiny. I believe that spiritual healing was calling me my entire life. I remember getting messages from Spirit stating that I was a born healer. The truth is, I was embarrassed by this. I had seen images on television of a minister performing spiritual healing and being very flamboyant in his actions, so this idea of healing was something that did not appeal to me. However, Harry's way of healing is truly the most gracious spiritual moment you will ever know. It is calm and relaxing and doesn't require any movement. It is meditative and indeed healing, almost like Reiki, but less complicated.

The healing course was something I was scared to do because Samantha told me it would release any old emotions I may have, and that this would make me a better medium. Despite my fear, I registered for this course, which would be under Harry's tutorial, scheduled for the fall of 2016. As I was told by the old crone, spiritual healing was something that I was born to do. What I have learned during my various training is that Spirit is the one in charge when it comes to your mediumship, healing, or psychic abilities.

I remember the week leading up to the healers' course, I was nervous because of what Samantha told me. However, brave as I was, I registered for this course. The course was to take place in the country, out of town, a tranquil space perfect for a healing environment. I volunteered to pick up some students from Switzerland who were arriving to our country for the course. I was excited because it made me feel like I had a purpose. I remember as we arrived at the retreat centre for our healing course, it was a spiritual moment full of possibilities. That is how I felt.

We checked into our rooms and then walked over to our first class which was meditation. The theme of the event was "surrender to spirit". We would each go up to the alter and light a candle to signify you were surrendering yourself to the spirit world. This was to make you a better spiritual healer. I remember going up to the altar and lighting my candle and saying a prayer. In this prayer I stated that I wanted to release my life to the spiritual world and for Spirit to help guide me. It was then that Spirit took over my life, and, like the phoenix, set fire to my old life.

The next class was Magnetic Healing. I remember vividly my very first magnetic healing. It was as if Spirit lit me up as from an electric plug. I was astounded by this experience to such a degree that it changed my life. As a result, I now understand energy and vibration in a professional sense of the word as related to Spirit and mediumship. The following class was contact healing. My very first contact healing experience was a trance healing session for me, which I did not know about at the time. I had had a minimal idea as to what "trance" was. I certainly was not aware there was such a thing called trance mediumship. Little did I know that I am a trance healer. The course I took was a 5-day healing course, and I was already an advanced healer, and no one told me.

When it came time to perform our first contact healing, I was already in touch with Spirit from meditation and the magnetic healing. As I stood behind my client, who was sitting on a chair in front of me, I called on my guides, guardians, and loved ones from another realm to help me with this healing. I said this in my mind. That is something I was taught at my mediumship circle. Then, I imagined my soul stepping out of my human body. I virtually unzipped my human energy body as I did that, I had a vision of my soul stepping out, relaxing on a couch beside me. I was "checked out," so to speak. Then my grandfather's spirit arrived, (my mother's dad). His spirit stepped inside my body as if he were real. I felt spirit step into my body and take over the healing. When spirit was finished, they stepped back out, and my soul stepped back in. I was undoubtedly in an altered state, a state of which I was totally unaware. It was a definite half-conscious state. I had begun to realize that I was not just a healer but a trance healer.

Being new at the healing modality, I was a bit confused as to why there was no one else in the class having the same experience as me. I was blown away. I remember telling some of the students in the class about my experience. Then I stopped because I could sense their energy of jealousy.

One person in the class stated, "Wow, I wish I had that." It was then that I decided not to share my experience with the class because I thought that Harry would think I was trying too hard to be the star student, so I simply kept quiet. I wished now that I would have discussed this with him because maybe he could have given me some clarity regarding my skills and left me better prepared mentally for all this new energy that I was acquiring.

The rest of the healer's course was very relaxed. We spent a lot of time in contemplation and meditation. It was superb. I needed it because I was still very emotional. What I did not realize was that I had opened Pandora's box at the start of the healer's course when I surrendered to spirit. During this healing course, we would meditate daily for about one and-a-half hours spread out throughout the day. During one meditation, Spirit showed me the room in which I was raped. In my meditation, this room was empty, and I was that little girl. I was in this room all by myself, and my older self came into the room and rescued me. That was one of the most vivid meditations ever. I was so deep in a trance that I forgot about the world and did not want to come back to myself.

Not long after that meditation, I started to have memories of my rape from when I was 12 years old, and from when I was sexually assaulted at the age of 48. These were nightmares and a flood of emotions that I could not control, all while trying to do a spiritual healing course. I remember leaving in the middle of one course exercise, in tears because I could not control my emotions. I had to walk away. Harry saw me leave and said nothing to me. These emotions were new and unfamiliar. It was the start of my life in terms of opening Pandora's box. I received a virtual key and opened up the memories that I had long since forgotten. It would be the start of chaos, torment, and the unwinding of myself and my life. I was a mess. Everything became unleashed. It was genuinely like a Pandora's box had been opened.

I did my best to get through the rest of the healer's course and told no one about my emotions that were becoming out of control. When I arrived back home, I did my best to forget about the emotions that were released. I volunteered to have two students from the healer's course stay with me for the night before their flight home, which was the next day. This would save them a stay in a hotel, as I had a beautiful guest room set up for visitors. We had a wonderful visit. They left for home the next day.

The healer's course transformed me somehow. I remember feeling different, like Spirit had changed me. I felt lighter and my soul felt at ease. It was as if my soul was aware of the release of Pandora's box and knew I was on a path of healing. At the very same time I felt emotionally unbalanced. It was bipolar mania that was starting to get the best of me. One moment I was elated, the next emotionally suicidal. Brandi had arranged to come and stay with me days later. I discussed with Brandi the truth of how I was feeling. I felt like I was able to do this for the first time in my life. I remember Brandi telling me that I was so emotionally unstable that if I worked a regular job, my emotions would affect it. She knew I was unraveling but did her best to stay out of the mess. By the mess I mean the massive ups and downs of my emotions. I remember Samantha coming to visit me, and Brandi was still there. Samantha was excited to find out how the healing course went and to see my new home. As I began to tell her how great it was, I burst into tears. I could not control my emotions any longer.

The truth of the matter was I did not understand why I was crying. I had never told Samantha about the rape. I was so messed up emotionally that I started to realize that I needed to talk to someone. Since the healing course, I was unstable emotionally, so Brandi thought the teachers should be made aware of how unraveled I had become as a result of their course. I did not realize that I was mentally ill with bipolar.

I agreed to contact Harry not only because he was my mediumship and healing teacher, but because he was a trained psychologist, my spiritual minister, and most of all, I thought of him as a mentor and friend. I trusted that he was more than capable of helping and referring me to someone if needed. I thought that in my soul Harry would have my best interests at heart. I felt I needed someone to help me who understood the mind of a medium, not just an ordinary muggle, (a muggle is someone who is non-magical). However, I was embarrassed, so instead of contacting Harry at church, I contacted him on Facebook Messenger because we were friends on that social media platform. I told him that I was an emotional mess after the healing course, that my rape memories had been released and that these new memories were starting to haunt me. I told him that I needed someone to speak to.

Brandi and Samantha left to go back to Alberta. I was scared to discuss the rape memories with Harry, so I did retail therapy to push my feeling down like I was used to. I did what I knew best and that was to go shopping. I impulsively purchased a seven-day retreat to Mexico at a resort. It was something that could make me feel better. I was scheduled to go to Mexico two weeks after I got out of the healing course. During this time, I had nightmares of the rape. Engaging in meditation would often unlock buried memories, bringing forth recollections I had long forgotten.

Harry agreed to meet me before the meditation and healing event that Thursday night at the church. In the meeting, Harry and I were strictly professional. I went to him as a psychologist, and he came to me as a friend. We never went into detail at all, which surprised me. The meeting lasted only 20 minutes at most. What we talked about was nothing earth-shattering and nothing was resolved as a result. I remember also stating to Harry that my mediumship was becoming out of control. I did not want to tell him that I was talking to him via telepathy, but I wanted to open the door to this conversation. I mentioned that my mediumship was becoming increasingly unmanageable, yet Harry completely ignored this aspect. Harry told me that I had pent up emotions that I had never faced. He agreed that a trip to Mexico would do me good. We agreed that if I needed him again that I would be able to contact him for another meeting. The meeting was short and sweet. There was no referral to a psychologist or counselor, so I thought I was doing well. It was this meeting that was the pivotal moment of this entire situation.

I knew enough back then to go for help. I went to an expert. Someone who was not just a psychologist but a medium, someone who would be able to help me with my mediumship which was becoming out of control. He was someone who was my teacher, who was training me to work with my mind through spiritual mediumship. When this started to become difficult to manage, I knew enough to go for help. And I did, to who I thought was the right person.

After the meeting was over, I remember going to the meditation and healing event at the church that night. Harry led us in a beautiful meditation. In that meditation, I started to go into a trance, and it was then that I saw a pier by a lake. At the end of this pier sat a little boy. I saw him sitting there.

I realized I too was just a little girl. I remember walking on this pier, and the little boy came up and said, "Hi, my name is Harry." I remember this like it was yesterday. It was vivid, just like the day I saw Harry in my head when my father died. This time it was so clear that I was being brought back to my inner child, and Harry was going to show me how to heal. I opened my eyes, and I saw Harry staring at me. It was surreal. It was times like these that made it difficult not to believe that I was talking to Harry in my mind. I always did my best to brush these thoughts aside and move on with my life.

The fact of the matter was that I needed to discuss my mediumship with Harry because it was perplexing me. It was to the point of causing me anguish and despair. I wish that back then I would have pressured Harry to discuss my mediumship in detail which would have led me telling him about the telepathy and my emotions. However, I sensed that Harry may not have been fully engaged when I sought his assistance. Following his response in our meeting, I opted to handle my emotions internally. I genuinely believed that seeking Harry for a psychology session would provide me with the solutions to my concerns, leading me to contemplate escaping to Mexico as a means of moving on from it all. I trusted Harry with the virtual key to the Pandora's box.

As the time went on, I had a difficult time dealing with life. I was glad that I had booked the trip to Mexico. However, even though the seven-day retreat was supposed to be restful, all I wanted to do was to curl up under a rock and die a slow death in the hot sun. I was having nightmares about my rape while I was there, and all seemed lost to me. Looking back, my undiagnosed bipolar was out of control. I remember being talked into a timeshare at the airport on the way to Mexico. I was undoubtedly manic. After all, this is not about purchasing a simple chocolate bar at a checkout counter. It is making big decisions which greatly affect your life. When I arrived home, I had my assistant cancel the timeshare. Beforehand, I had prided myself on being spontaneous. Looking back now, I can see that it was bipolar mania which fueled these actions. The decisions that I made have affected my entire life, decisions such as moving to this new city and leaving my business behind. Now, going to Mexico and buying a timeshare that I could not afford was something that proved to be more than just spontaneous. It was affecting my life on a grand scale. What I did to alleviate this issue was to bury my emotions under the rubble of the storm that had not finished passing. I buried these emotions and poured myself into working hard to expand my company and working hard in my church studies.

During this time, life became complicated with my overbearing emotions. The rape memories were all-consuming. I could not handle them. I needed to do something to keep my mind busy. The solution was to build another company to bury my emotions. I decided to start a charity for rape victims called Pandora's Box. It was a charity for victims who were beginning to heal. It would be for people who were ready to move on with their life and who needed help. It was a charity to motivate people in their personal growth and development and to make over their life in a positive way. I was to be the first candidate. I had sponsors for each candidate that would include a life coach, a therapist, a health and wellness expert, a motivational coach, a business/career coach, and more. Each candidate would participate for one year. The idea was to inspire and motivate, and to help people change their life in a more positive direction.

During this year, with being the Director and the first candidate, I was to showcase my progress through videos. These videos would be on YouTube and the website. The sponsors would advise people via videos that were available on our website in order to help them evolve and move past the hurt and the pain. It was a large-scale charity which would launch in January of 2017. I felt that it was something unique and much needed. I wanted to be better than I was—I wanted to help people move past the hurt. It was all set to launch on social media. It had all been professionally done, much like a movie premiere. I had a professional movie trailer created to introduce Pandora's Box. I had all the sponsors lined up and ready to go. Pandora's Box helped me forget about the emotions that I had buried. I was so happy rebuilding my new life.

I messaged Harry about this charity, but I did not hear back from him. I continued with my life as if I were mentally healthy. I started to lose weight. I showcased my weight loss on video and wanted to talk about the eating disorder that had resulted from my rape. I had eaten because of my trauma. Food gave me love when I needed it the most. I wanted to showcase to the world how such a tragedy can affect your entire life. Therefore, with

Pandora's Box, one could heal and start over again. Building Pandora's Box helped me to understand the emotions that were coming at me. I looked forward to seeing the therapist the most. With her, I could sort myself out the best way I knew how. I tried reaching out to Harry again to see what his reaction was, and he did not respond. He ignored my messages.

I had a few months before the release of Pandora's Box, and I used it to plan the execution of this newfound charity carefully. I used my time wisely. I slept very little. I would mostly work on projects. I am a project person. I work best when I am working towards something. The other task I was working on was rebuilding all my salons for them to be streamlined, so that I could franchise the system that I had developed. I wanted to grow them across Canada. It was feasible because I had 13 salons at that time as I had sold three of them to help me move to British Columbia. It was a busy time for me. One of the most significant contracts I had was with 7 of my salons, and this was going up for tender (a contract/lease renewal) in June of 2017. As a result, I was using all my abilities to make the salons even better than they currently were. I worked extremely hard to ensure my success rate of maintaining my salon contracts/leases. To avoid my emotions, I worked like a workaholic. I worked on streamlining everything in my personal and business life, and this was something that I was good at.

During the planning phase of Pandora's Box and franchising my business, I still found time for my spirituality and my friends from the church. I remember Hilda telling me that I needed help and that she could not be my friend if I did not get it. She added that it was something that she currently could not deal with. It was because I told her about my rape, and she told me that she, too, was sexually abused by a friend's uncle. She told me that she could not remember specific events of this incident. Neither of us was prepared to deal with this pain, so we separated as friends. We saw each other in church and at the Sunday morning coffee before church. It felt to me that everything was going wrong again because of my emotions. I was starting to realize that I could not hide from them. At the same time, one of my sisters took ill and was in the hospital, and we were not sure if she was going to make it. I had a lot on my plate and needed to keep a solid grasp on reality. I tried extremely hard to keep a level head, but one day at church Minister

Tanis came up to me and asked me how I was doing. I burst into tears, but my emotional outburst went unacknowledged, brushed aside once more.

I could not hide from my emotions. I was starting to be overly emotional all the time. What saved me from going crazy back then was my home. I was lucky in terms of where I lived because it was right by the ocean, and I could walk to it. The ocean grounded me. My landlady and I were relatively close, and when it came time to pay her rent, we would drink champagne together and have appetizers. Rental payday was always a fun time for us both. My landlady had researched me before I moved in and saw on my LinkedIn social media profile that I was a powerhouse businesswoman. She too was a great businesswoman back in her day, so we had a lot in common. She was trying to convince me to join her women's group which consisted of high society women from all over the city. I was seriously considering this as I felt it would give me a leg up in the expansion of my company to British Columbia, Canada.

Soon fall became winter and I was scheduled to go to Martin and Mandy's for New Years that year. Martin had agreed to interview me about Pandora's Box in time for my opening video to be released on January 1st, 2017. I had all the sponsors ready to start. I would begin going to a therapist as part of the plan. It set my mind at ease to know that someone would be there to listen to my troubles. I was aware of how much trauma and grief I had been through, but I had no one to understand just how much chaos there was happening for me. Harry appeared reluctant to address my concerns, and I interpreted his response as an indication that I might be relatively fine since he seemed to dismiss it. Given his roles as both a psychologist and a medium, and our existing familiarity, I placed trust in him. The reassurance came from the belief that if there were any issues, he would openly communicate them to me. The other therapist was strictly for chats to clear up the little emotions. That is what I thought.

I set off to transform my life and be the role model that others would aspire to be. I started with ten sponsors. They were all ready to go for our launch. As the Pandora's Box charity commenced, I was also set to take a weekly mediumship course with Harry. I again sent Harry a message about Pandora's Box, and he did not respond. It was as if he had wiped his hands of me. I was given permission to enroll in his private mediumship class. The course was rumoured to have a 2-year waiting list. I did not have to wait, so that was exciting. Harry knew about my mediumship blowing up and getting out of control, and he still allowed me into the class. I was ecstatic.

While I waited for the course to begin, I continued working on my charity, my business and myself. I wanted to start the Pandora's Box charity to help motivate myself. I wanted to get out of the hole that I had found myself in. To tell the truth, I was not sure what was happening to me, but I felt relieved to know that my new friends from the spiritual church would be there to help me if needed. I was getting close to this community of friends. They helped me get through a very difficult time in my life.

This leads me to the topic of support when you are bipolar. If you have the support of people who are aware of the disorder, then all is possible. You can get through it without ruining your life. Without proper support, it is hopeless. My situation should not have been hopeless because I thought I had friends and family who would help. I understand now that mental illness needs more awareness. People are afraid to talk about mental illness. There is a shame factor that goes along with discussing mental illness. What can hurt even more is watching someone lose their life entirely. The spiritual community that knew me watched me destroy my life. I had the proper support around me such as a trained psychologist who was my friend, mentor and mediumship teacher.

Chapter Nine- The Roller Coaster Ride

At this point in my journey, life felt great because I was obliviously manic. During the weeks of the Pandora's Box's launch, I felt like I was starting to heal my past. I started to have a jam-packed calendar. I woke every morning at 5:00am. I meditated for one hour, had a protein shake, then worked out at the gym with a personal trainer. I then went home, got ready for work, and to keep me on track, I met daily with my sponsors. The goal of Pandora's Box was to motivate people who had been compromised. I needed the motivation to move on. Pandora's Box was there to fill a void in my life. It was also there to inspire others who needed help.

In one sense life felt fulfilled again. I felt like this would be the new start that I needed. However, the underlying demons were pushing me into a rabbit hole. During the third week into the charity, I met my assistant for lunch. She asked me how I felt. I told her that I felt like I should go to the hospital. I felt so bad. Not one thing was physically wrong with me, but I felt terrible. I could not explain why, except to say that my entire body was consumed with grief, terror, uncertainty, uncontrolled emotions, and more. I kept moving forward with my life the best I could after this. That is when things get blurry. The emotions that I was feeling were real and serious. However, I was ignoring them all because I was mentally ill.

I was going to my weekly mediumship course with Harry then, which made me happy, and I was better than ever at my mediumship. I went to congregant studies at church, and Martin and Mandy were helping me study—they too were registered for the course. That night they were to stay at my house. I felt so consumed with Spirit during this time. Harry was communicating with me in spirit through telepathy, or so I thought. The truth was I was starting to enter into psychosis, and I did not know. There is a fine line between mediumship and psychosis. Through mediumship, one may experience visions and perceive the whispers of spirits. In contrast, with psychosis, delusions may manifest visually, and voices may be heard. A fine line indeed. That is why I chose to see Harry for help—because of his specialty.

I would stay in bed meditating for over 14 hours per day, only waking up for the essentials of life. I had hallucinations of Harry performing hypnotherapy on me for my rape memories. I started to have a clear recollection of the time when I was raped. It became clear to me what had happened and I knew in my soul that it made sense. Then one day I started to have delusions as well. Deep within my soul lies a turmoil I have never talked about to anyone until now. When I was deep in my psychosis and manic, I had something similar to a lucid dream, but closer to a hallucination or delusion of Harry telling me that someone dear to my heart had raped me as well as raped my mother and one of my sisters. It was so vivid. This was not mediumship at all. It was psychosis. It was not true at all, but in my mind, I thought it was true. I started to get what I thought were memories of this terrible event. The voices were telling me that I had been raped and described how I was raped and so I started to believe it. The truth is I had been raped but not by someone near and dear to me. My mother and sister had never been raped. It was a delusion. I was also told that this rape reoccurred until I reached my adult years. The terrifying thing was that I believed this to be true. I did not realize truth at that time.

This was a very confusing time for me. I started to believe that my entire life was a lie. How could it possibly be that this person who was dear to me would do this and that everyone in the family buried this fact? I felt lost at sea so to speak. I thought that everything in my life had been a lie and that was the part that broke me. I had started to understand my actual rape when I was 12 years old at the house party, but I was confused at this new realization that someone dear to me had also raped me. I felt as if my life were over because how could I go on knowing that my life had been a lie? I was torn between two worlds—two lifetimes. It was a living nightmare. It was so vivid that it consumed me.

Martin and Mandy were my house guests one night. That night I awoke with such vivid dreams, hallucinations and delusions of Harry telling me that I was being raped by someone near and dear to me. I woke up Mandy and

Martin, who were in the next room, Martin, feeling uncomfortable, went back to bed, and let Mandy take care of me. I was so distraught. I told Mandy everything, including the fact that "I knew Harry was helping me through telepathy". I told her that the dream stated that I had been raped repeatedly until my adult years. When we awoke the next morning, I was still upset, and I asked Mandy and Martin to speak to Harry about what was happening to me. I thought that Harry could help shed some light on this for me, and then I would come clean about him helping me through telepathy. Mandy and Martin left, having agreed to speak to Harry and get back to me. No one made a move to come and help me. I expected Harry to come and see me at my house after Martin and Mandy telling him how mentally unhealthy I was or, at the very least, I thought someone from the church would come help me. No one called or came to visit me or referred me to a mental health professional. I was so upset. The overall situation lacked the compassion and empathy I needed from my friends. I had a breakdown and it lasted too long.

Just like that, I stopped my entire world. I stopped going to church, to my classes, and I dropped my Pandora's Box charity schedule and my sponsors. I thought I was going to die. I felt like I was being tormented in my mind. Other feelings were also there. I sensed Spirit around me, inside my body. I can see now that Spirit came to heal me. I was in the virtual rabbit hole, my Pandora's box, my phoenix ready to be burned. I was a mess. A magic carpet ride from Spirit was about to begin. I was on the crazy train that Ozzy sang about. The turmoil from my past had finally captured me. I felt consumed with grief. It was like I had a heart attack, but I hadn't. That feeling lasted for days. I remember the rest in bits and pieces. I do not remember anybody from the church community calling to find out where I was. I remember the police coming to my door. They were called by the church, to see if I was ok. It sent shock waves through my landlady. It started to cause a rift between us because she was afraid of what the neighbors would say because of the police vehicle outside of her house. It was then that I decided to start to drop out of society.

I could not believe that none of my friends had come to see me from the church or my Pandora's Box charity. This was so cold and callous to me. I made a drastic move. I gave my cell phone to my assistant and obtained a new phone and gave no one my new number, not even my family or my friend Maple. When Maple found out that I changed my phone number she somehow reached me and told me to go get an exorcism. This was similar to the movie the Exorcist, which is an old movie about a young girl who had been possessed by demons. I could not believe this was coming out of her mouth. I chose to stay away from her at that point.

I wanted someone from the church to help because they were the ones who trained me to work with my mediumship brain. I thought being a medium, they would understand my situation better. I felt quite distressed that even Martin, Mandy, and Hilda didn't check in on me. Despite being in regular contact with most of them every week, the fact that I withdrew from social interactions and not a single person came to check on me still surprises me to this day. That is where my heart started to break. I had put all my efforts into going to the church, and they could not take the time to come and see if I was ok after knowing about the trauma and grief that I had endured. I needed help other than the usual form of help. I did not need a "muggle". I needed someone who had a "medium mind" and a psychology degree to help me sort out the ability that they had trained me in. Harry was that person, but he had been standoffish at our only visit when he had counseled me months before. I did not go back to see him, and I now needed him the most. He would not arrive.

When your mind goes berserk from being manic and from psychosis it is so subtle that it feels normal, at least it did for me. I am a spiritual medium and I listen for the faint whispers and thoughts that are Spirit. When your mind goes rogue you do not really notice it at first. You feel like you just came out of meditation. You feel like that all the time. You are on a natural high and it is something that feels wonderful when the moods are up, but when the moods are down that is another story. The down times are like going through what hell could possibly be like, maybe worse. I remember sitting in bed for hours upon hours during the day and just listening to the voices in my mind. It was entertaining to say the least. It was like being in a horror film and being the star of that film.

Then I started to listen to the voices. This is how everything became so messed up. I listened to them and when it did not work out the way the voices said it would, it sent me into a deeper depression. I had suicidal thoughts. The transition from being mentally healthy to mentally insane is very subtle. I was not one to anger easily. I was both a higher and lower version of myself. To look at me you would not realize that I was mentally ill. I looked normal and no one had any idea that I was crippled inside. It can be very lonely when you are mentally ill because I hid the truth about what was happening to me. The only one I had told was Harry. My mediumship ability went from average to absurd. I made a mediumship chart on the different categories of spirits who would come my way. It was all based on their vibration, whether high, low, or medium. It was a turbulent and nonsensical time.

I can now understand why Harry felt so safe to me. I was away from my home that I had known for 48 years and suddenly found myself in a strange province with strangers. This was something that I had never imagined could happen. It was too much change for me. There was so much grief, loss, and pain running through my veins and it became too much. It all becomes too much when one goes into psychosis. It can happen during a change such as a divorce, a move to a different city, a death etc. I am sure this is not the first case of someone losing their mind and I am sure that it will not be the last. I went into such a deep depression, I wanted to end my life. I had nothing to live for. I got rid of all the memories—photos, trinkets, anything that reminded me of my old life. I felt that I had been deceived. I got rid of all my books from the Church and all my mementos. All the beautiful memories I had were gone. I gave my duties to my assistant, so she left me alone. I had no one to talk to during this time. I was so perplexed.

I remember sending Harry a message stating that I needed to talk to him. It was on Facebook Messenger. In the message I left him my phone number. When he called, I was by the ocean. I remember answering the phone, and when we spoke, he asked how he could help. I simply said— "I Love You." I was clearly psychotic, unbeknownst to me. Just a simple I love you. Then I said that someone near and dear had raped me. He responded that I would have to be supervised by a female minister if I ever wanted to see him. I vaguely remember him telling me he would refer me to a psychologist, but he never did. The rest of the conversation is fuzzy to me. I was extremely unstable emotionally with no one around to help. If I am perfectly honest, I did love Harry on a soul level. If I had been mentally stable, I would have never mentioned 'I Love you' because it was indeed inappropriate. But at the time I was mentally ill.

I waited a few days and did not hear from Harry. I was then told by the voices in my head to show up at his house. It made sense to go to his home, because I wanted to stay at home and commit suicide but somewhere within, I wanted to reach out for help. I honestly thought he was the person who could help me sort out this situation. I remember driving aimlessly down the road in busy traffic trying to remember where Harry lived. I stubbornly drove for hours in my delusional state. I drove into his driveway, walked up the stairs and knocked on the door. I was calm on the outside but on the inside, it was as if my soul had been ripped out of my body. I was scared stiff. Harry opened the door and looked appalled that I had come to his house. He seemed angry. I asked him if we could talk, and he agreed to talk at the church. I drove to the church and waited for him to arrive. He arrived with the female minister Tanis and one other male minister. They seated themselves behind a long boardroom table. They wanted me to sit across from them. It was a profoundly severe intervention. They all appeared incredibly angry. I picked up on their feelings and felt like I did not belong in their church anymore. I recognized that they were angry about the visit to Harry's house and the love comment.

I was surprised by the way I was being treated. I was not a crazed love stalker. I was a student and church congregant of his who was having a mental health crisis and I needed his help. I had gone to his house instead of staying at home and committing suicide. I had entrusted him with the most profound and darkest moment of my life, and he let me down. The only person who spoke was Harry, and he asked why I was there. I replied that he had been talking to me via telepathy. I went on to say that the secret code that Spirit told me to give him was Operation 30. I thought that would get his attention and tell him that the telepathy was real but it did not. He told me he knew nothing of this telepathy and of Operation 30. Harry did not blink and told me that I was in psychosis and that I needed to go to mental health emergency immediately. His delivery was blunt and lacked warmth. I thought that I was okay, especially given the results of my prior meeting with him. I was severely in denial. I very politely walked away from them and left the building. I expected someone to run after me to get me to understand that what I was doing was wrong. However, no one came after me, and no one in this community called or came to help. At the time I did not know what psychosis was. I thought Harry was being absurd. I felt that he was angry at me for telling him that I loved him.

Being sent to mental health emergency is like the movie One Flew Over the Cuckoo's Nest starring Jack Nicholson. In the film, nurse Ratched tormented the main character. This was not a particularly good image that I have of mental health support. So when I heard the words psychosis and hospital, I graciously declined. Days later, the police came to see me again. They told me to stay away from Harry's house and that they wanted to ensure that I was ok. Everything was becoming a blur to me, and the days rolled into one. I was consumed by the memories of my actual rape and the delusion of the other rapes.

That following week, I dropped out of society even further. I did not deal with business, friends, family, or anything for several weeks. However, I was always looking at my email, as this felt the safest way to communicate for me. Then one morning at two o'clock, there was a knock at the door, and my sister from Alberta was at my doorstep. She had been called by the Church. They had my friend Maple's phone number from the church application as an emergency contact. The church had called Maple to get my sister's phone number to come and see me and to get me help. My sister was aware that I went to Harry's house and simply told me to stay away from him and the Church. I had mastered being calm, and I convinced my sister that I was perfectly fine, because at the time I honestly thought I was ok. She tried to convince me to see a doctor for mental stress. This surprised me because I thought that I was in perfect condition. I honestly thought that my mind was sick because of a mediumship issue, something that I could only share with a mediumship professional. Mental illness was never brought up in our mediumship studies. I feel it should have been. After spending a week with me, my sister reluctantly left to go back home.

The church did not call to see if I was ok. I did receive an email from Tanis stating that if I wanted to go to the church that I needed to first see a psychiatrist. I was horrified by this, and I felt shamed. At one point I do remember Harry messaging me on Facebook telling me I was welcome to go to church but that he was off limits. I wanted to talk to Harry, and he was not available to me. I then started to contact Harry via social media and email to get him to evaluate my mediumship skills. This was all I thought I needed at that time. I brushed the rape under the carpet and chose to focus on the voices in my head. However, Harry called the police on me to get me to stop contacting him. The police came to visit about five times, and I crashed even further.

The nightmares of my rape were too much to bear. This period of time was like an inferno, a massive fire dangerously out of control. During this time, the police warned me against contacting Harry and cautioned that if I continued, I would be charged with criminal harassment. I was too mentally ill to understand the repercussions of this. When Harry did not want to help me, I became frustrated and tried even harder to get him to understand. So I emailed him pages and pages of writings that I would compile to get him to understand what was happening to me. When that did not work, I created videos of Spirit communicating with me. What it was at that time was psychosis mixed with mediumship. Harry still did not help. He only sent the police to see me yet again, this time trying to get me to go to the hospital for an assessment. I declined. It all became too much to handle.

I believed that a minister should, at the very least, demonstrate compassion and assist me in obtaining the help I sought. The intervention orchestrated by Harry and the other ministers turned out to be frightening, intimidating, and shocking, lacking the compassion one would expect from a minister. The involvement of the police added to the fear for both myself and my landlady. Unable to reach Harry, I contemplated ending my life, feeling that everything had spiraled into a complete and utter lie. My intention was not to seek attention; I genuinely felt overwhelmed and believed ending my life was the only solution amidst the chaos.

In the meantime, I was still running my business with the help of my assistant. It was then that I needed to work on my proposal to renew seven of my salon contracts, as they were going up for tender in June of 2017. The submission for the proposal was due in a few weeks. It was terrible timing. When you are bipolar without support, it makes it challenging to manage your life, not to mention your business. It was proving to be impossible to manage my business successfully. My assistant did not know my business as I did. What I needed was a support system to help me with my business and life. Money was not coming in like it was going out. I was not managing the finances carefully. I had my inheritance money from my father that I was saving for my retirement which I was spending to keep me afloat. I was not thinking of the future at all, because my thought process was that I would be dead soon.

In general, I was good at business. I had grown two companies, and they had initially been successful. I can look back now and see that it was impossible to manage all this without support. The business was slowly going down the drain because of my mental illness. I had no one to catch my fall. I was ill and needed help. The resources that had once been available to me were no longer within reach, leaving me to confront this brain health issue entirely on my own.

My mind felt shattered from its illness. The nightmares continued to consume me and set me off course to what I call the crazy train. I look back and understand how mixed up everything was. I was crying every night. I had no idea at this time that it would only get worse. I was confused and brushed everything off as nothing.

Chapter Ten- Backstage Pass to Spirit

Suicidal tendencies run deep when you are bipolar, but Spirit helped to detract me from this. However, there was sorrow and trauma that was seeping out of my mind, body, and soul. Spirit seemed so present as if it were real. I remember listening to music, and it was like I was inside the song. I could hear every music note as it spoke to my soul. It catapulted me into something unreal. The mania mixed with psychosis moments were the absolute best. They were the moments when I was out of touch with the realities of life, and I had no clue. It detracted me from all the pain. Spirit poured over my body like purple rain. Purple, the color of Spirit, was the color I was surrounded in. Purple is a pure spiritual color, a color of the crown chakra where Spirit communicates through you. Spirit was indeed communicating with me. It was the darkest moment of my life, but the most intense spiritually. I was a spiritual medium in a spiritual crisis.

I remember listening to the song Purple Rain for hours upon hours. I have come to realize that this song is spiritual. I remember praying to the Great Spirit. I felt peace when thinking of the song. In my pain and sorrow, I captured every note that played, and it brought me peace. I went into oblivion, and I was captivated by Spirit's essence. The timeline and events of life during this period are fuzzy for me. However, I remember Spirit very clearly. I was distraught, and Spirit entertained my soul. I remember being in a trance state, and I was being taken over by a spirit. I would use all my clair senses to communicate with this spirit. The time was a manic all-time high. Words would come out of my mouth that I would not normally speak. It was spirit talking through my mouth. I was trance channeling spirit without knowing what I was doing. Spirit worked through me seamlessly. Spirit entered my body and used it to speak and to move. It came at a challenging time, a time when I was unaware of what was happening to me. At that time,

I did not realize I was bipolar or manic. I simply shut out the fact that Harry had told me that I was in psychosis.

Mediumship made my life extremely challenging at this time. It caused me to become further estranged from the people I loved. It was because the mediumship was mixed with mania. All my senses were heightened at this time. I was channeling spirits who were celebrities as well as loved ones, friends, and people who I did not know. The time was very mystical. Much like in the tarot cards, I was the fool embarking on a soul's journey. This time was esoteric. It was mystical and scary at the same time. Spirit was becoming my haven.

When I realized that I was back to reality, it left me with a feeling of emptiness and hopelessness. My life was in turmoil, and I had dropped out of society. Life had sent me on a magic carpet ride which proved to be very intoxicating. It was the start of the hero's journey. That is when a hero goes on an adventure and after an unsettling crisis, wins a victory and comes home transformed. It is like this when you live a life of spirituality, and you learn from it. It was just the beginning. I thought things would work out one moment, and the next I would be in despair.

What helped me from committing suicide was that Spirit came in and introduced me to my 'Collective Souls'. Much like Esther Hicks channels Abraham, I was channeling the Collective Souls. They are spirit that have evolved over time. Spirit told me that when we pass over, our energy continues to carry on. That we remain who we were on earth but without our physical body. Over time we continue to evolve spiritually, therefore helping us become the best that we were meant to be. Spirit continued to tell me that once we are fully evolved, we collect together. Our energies combine into what some call God, Source Energy or the Great Spirit etc. Once we collect together into our fully evolved self, we are then the 'Collective Souls'. I was channeling the Collective Souls.

The start of the collective soul channeling was the purest spiritual moment of my life. It may seem absurd, or hilarious but it was infact very fulfilling spiritually to know that Spirit is real, and that the universe certainly does have our back. That Spirit guides us by way of our intuition and gut instinct. The only thing that stood in my way of being a successful medium during that time was bipolar, mania and psychosis. Nonetheless, I can't help but believe that this mental illness actually allowed me to fully relax and unwind, enabling spirit communication to occur at its best. I was not brought up to be religious or spiritual. Spirit found me and captured me. Spirit had been trying to contact me my entire life. It was a 'spiritual calling' and I finally answered.

I was so oblivious to the world that Spirit came in full throttle. It was the start of the backstage pass, an all-access pass into the spirit world. Prince introduced my spirit team as the "Collective Souls." The Collective Souls are people who have passed on. I was channeling spirit, but not just any spirit. These were celebrities and people who had passed on and who were from every walk of life. However, it did not stop there. It was majestic. It was a beautiful time which was known as trance channeling. The Collective Souls taught me to become connected to my Higher Power, my inner child, and to channel the Great Spirit. I was manic and delusional when Spirit came to help me. I had unraveled my soul understanding, and it changed my life. Spirit gave me a feeling of peace and hope when I needed it the most. It guided me to not give up. It told me to keep going, no matter what. The Collective Souls gave me advice on spirit, life, vibration, and alignment. This experience changed my life.

My Collective Souls came in one by one, Prince, Audrey Hepburn, Marilyn Monroe, James Dean, Nina Simone, Elizabeth Taylor, Louis Armstrong, Dean Martin, Frank Sinatra, Sammy Davis Jr., Johnny Cash, Janice Joplin, Roy Orbison, Jim Croce, Elvis, Michael Jackson, Freddy Mercury, Buddy Holly, and Elizabeth Montgomery, to name a few. With all my senses of a medium, I was able to connect in a way I never had before. I was in a full trance-mediumship state. The time was surreal, and it was like I was in the spirit world with Spirit. It was like I had ascended my vibration so high, that my level of consciousness was beyond anything I could imagine. I started to bring in Spirit full time. I had stopped my world entirely, and I became engrossed in Spirit. I was oblivious to what was going on around me. During this time, I would meditate for hours and talk to Spirit out loud. It was a distraction from dealing with the emotions that came flooding in from the delusions.

I was so vibrationally high that Spirit came through in such an extremely powerful way. I felt like I was in trance state all the time. During my manic phase, all my Claire senses were activated. I would often do my spiritual channeling in front of the mirror or I would video myself to hear and see my face and how it became altered. This sensation sent shock waves through me. I could see Spirit in my face. I was channeling spirit in a much grander sense of the word. It is a certainty that we, as spiritual mediums, provide messages from spirit to the living ones left behind. It is not so different to understand that I was channeling celebrities. After all, if I can get a stranger's loved one's message from spirit on a spiritual stage show presentation, I am more than capable of performing the backstage pass.

The first celebrity to enter my humble abode that night was Prince. I was told by Prince that Spirit arrived to help people evolve. As I trance channeled Prince, I saw him like he was real. He would come when I was eating and tell me to eat healthier and showed me how to cook in a healthy way. His presence was evident, and I felt I knew him just as I would in a proper mediumistic message on the platform. I felt his slender body. I felt that he was enlightened as a human. I felt that he was an absolute rock star, that he had attitude and was full of life. However, he took crap from no one. He was a male version of a diva, but kind at the same time. I felt his emotions while I played his songs, and I took on his body movements as if I were him. It was as if every motion felt like Prince was the one doing the movements. Looking back, it is still amazing to me how real the event seemed. It was much like the 80's movie "Heart and Souls" with the actor Robert Downey Junior. In the film, the spirit enters the character's body, and he goes into a trance and takes on the personality and whole persona of the spirit. This is what happened to me.

Spirit mixed with mania helped my mind relax on a different vibrational level of consciousness. It helped me understand freedom from any crutches that normal life offered. My worries were gone. I was in oblivion, and Spirit was able to work through me to perfection. The thoughts of my life being a total sham were hidden beneath the wreckage from the virtual storm called mental illness. Time went fast, and the days rolled into one. Spirits came to me one by one. They came to see me because I was aware, mediumistically speaking. I was aware of the senses; it was a gift that Spirit had bestowed upon me. One night they were all in my room, and I could tell each one apart some by clairvoyance, and clairaudience, and others by claircognizance. As their energies were brought in, I could identify each one. When they came through, I could give proper spiritual medium evidence of their existence.

I felt the urge to play "Purple Rain," and the pivotal song "Let's Go Crazy." As Prince states in the song about life and the elevator, it was like the stairway to heaven. As he sang, the vibration was the truth that he, too, had come to understand the mystic art of the Great Spirit. I believe this was physical mediumship, something that I was not accustomed to. The best way I can describe physical mediumship is when the spirits take over your body, causing one to be in a storm. I felt each spirit come through to me in such a different way than I had before. I was in a mystical three-dimensional world, with spirit calling the shots.

The next Collective Soul to arrive was Audrey Hepburn. Audrey arrived as herself, then acted the part of Holly Golightly. This character was from one of my favorite movies, "Breakfast at Tiffany's." It was a peculiar situation for me because she strolled into my bedroom as a friend, and yet I was her fan. Then Audrey came as herself and was adamant that she was now Audrey, and not the character Holly. She came through as a sophisticated, quiet lady and Prince showed up as the rock star. The other star who came through was Marilyn Monroe. She came as Marilyn, not Norma Jean, to me. She told me that we are all brought together to help our souls evolve. The night was filled with music, physical trance mediumship, and information that I will never forget. I was sitting in a room full of stars. Through the night, one by one, the Collective Souls took turns entering my body, performing their platform mediumship and giving me messages about how to go on with my life. As the night went on with Prince, Audrey, and Marilyn, I would get a soul urge to play their favorite songs or clips from their movies on YouTube. It was like having a virtual mediumship evening. I would feel like the stars, sound like them, and act like them.

Frank Sinatra came through as a debonair class act who was a force to be reckoned with. We sang the song "New York, New York", and he showed me some fancy footwork and dance moves. It was as if I were a channel to the spirits, and one by one, they would come in, sometimes alone, sometimes together. Some stayed longer; some were very definitely there but briefly. James Dean was smart and gentle. I had the "Rat Pack" in my bedroom. Nina Simone, the famous blues singer, was very straightforward. She sang and moved just as she did in the YouTube videos I had looked up. It was a moment I will never forget. She talked about her life in a racist world. She was there to give me strength and courage. Louis Armstrong came, and yes, it is a wonderful world. He corrected me on how I said his name. I had his moves, his voice, and his era to an exact science.

Elizabeth Taylor came to me as a feisty woman who was self-assured and confident. We went shopping for beauty products together. She picked out a hair mousse and face cream that I would normally not have bought because they were way too expensive. I was manic and delusional and spent my money on odd things like that. She also came to me as the actress in "Cat on a Hot Tin Roof". This surprised me because I had never seen the movie. I had to look it up afterwards. When Dean Martin came through, we sang the song "That's Amore." I had champagne, and that helped me to relax. Johnny Cash came in with my father. He was a proud father who wanted to share with me who he had met in spirit. We sang "Hurt" and "Ring of Fire". Johnny Cash had been my father's favorite singer.

Janice Joplin came through, and we sang "Me and Bobby McGee" and "Mercedes Benz". It was like I had turned into Janice. I felt like I was the spitting physical image of her and that I had her voice to perfection. I have been told that living humans can help spirits evolve. When they arrive to see you, they help you evolve by sending you messages. This, in turn, helps them to evolve. I feel that Janice helped me to grow, as I felt her soul on a deep, passionate level. Prior to this, I had never been a fan of Janice Joplin's. It was a real soul calling. I felt that by Janice Joplin arriving, our vibrations matched, and we grew our vibrations to a higher level by feeling our way to a brighter light.

We also sang with John Lennon. He wanted to sing the song "Give Peace a Chance." It was evident that he was at peace, and his vibration was soft and calm. He was brought in at the end of the night to give me peace. As I was channeling such spirits in my bedroom, I was looking in the mirror and videotaping the event at the same time. I saw John Lennon's son's face in mine when we would play the song Give Peace a Chance. I knew his son was alive and well, so the capability of Spirit in this sense surprised me. It remains a mystery to me as to how real this was and what my mind was doing at the time to give me such clear, precise mediumship messages.

Roy Orbison's & Jim Croce's spirits arrived. They were some of the gentler spirits who would arrive. I know Jim Croce's songs well. However, he was a very distant but evident spirit. Channeling Roy Orbison and Jim Croce felt like mental mediumship. They were not feeling like three-dimensional spirits, nor was it trance, or physical. Elvis came to me as the middle-aged Elvis. I looked in the mirror during that time, and my face turned into his. It seemed real, and it was real for a few seconds that night. I kept the full-length mirror by my bed and would sit and look at it as I did my mediumship. Michael Jackson came through very softly and only by voice—no actions. My voice sounded like his. The next was Freddy Mercury who came in and taught me some dance moves as if he were really in the room. My Collective Souls vibration was high, they brought me happiness and tranquility.

At night, the spirits were different, very contrasting compared to my Collective Souls. Harry would bring in the 'secret society'. These were hallucinations that Harry, through telepathy, was bringing in his friends to meet me in spirit. I had known of these friends through various outlets. Some I had met. Others I saw on webpages and Facebook, and I knew they were mediums as well. During these mediumship events that some would call hallucinations, this group of gifted mediums told me that they were called the Secret Society. As each of these incarnate spirits arrived, I remember knowing the energy of each spirit who came to visit. There were so many that I can't remember all their names. In my mind, I was being initiated into this secret club. I was told in spirit that I was going to be initiated as Harry's first virtual reality mediumship student. The Society was comprised of elite people who were to remain nameless and in spirit only. I was channeling them all night. They came in one by one. I thought this was real so I posted a comment on Harry's Facebook page, stating that I was going to be his first virtual reality mediumship student. He did not respond to this.

The days would start as early as 6 am. The Secret Society of medium professionals was a private club that held the secret to life. At times, the communication from this spirit-lead secret society was cruel, much like being in a boot camp. The Secret Society tempted me daily to spend my money, and to drink, and eat. They would tell me disheartening things to beat me down and lower my morale. Then, they would call the police on me when I was at my lowest moment. Reality was mixed with spirit and this made this time of my life very messy. When the nights would end, my bipolar low started, and I caved. I was on a bipolar high when the Collective Souls would come through with the team of celebrities. A cluster of emotions were coming at me, and I was perplexed by it all.

When I was at my lowest, Spirit brought in the 'Helter Skelter Spirits', a mafia of dark spirits that came only when my mania vibration was low enough. I was also channeling spirits like Charles Manson. Manson taught me about lower vibration and how it affects you as a medium. These lower spirits were sometimes abusive in a vibrational sense of the word. There was a sense of darkness from these spirits. They seemed to be the voices of my childhood, events such as when I was bullied.

Next to arrive was the 'Spirit mafia'. I grew up never entirely watching the movie "The Godfather" or any other gangster mob movie but I had seen clips. Spirit came through and provided me with a force with which to deal with these dark-spirit bullies and to guard me against the terrible visions and awful nightmares. In proper form, Spirit brought in the spirit mafia. One of these was "Lucky Luciano", an actual gangster. This Spirit Mafia was going to knock the block off of anyone who dared to tread on my turf. They were my virtual bodyguards. I now understand that that it was a lesson on personal power. Nonetheless, the time was intense, and I was too sensitive. I understood all this to be real. Mania, psychosis, and mediumship had opened the gates of heaven and hell.

I contacted Harry at the church and pleaded for him to help me and to evaluate my mediumship. I believed that it was a mediumship issue which was blowing out of proportion, just as I had stated to him in our original meeting. What I did not understand was that this trance-style mediumship was also mixed with psychosis and mania.

Chapter Eleven- The Call to Adventure

The days surrounding the backstage pass were extremely exciting. I was chatting to Harry via telepathy, as well as chatting to my Collective Souls through my mediumship abilities turned psychosis. I was a busy gal. However, Harry had plans for me, and he was working collectively with the gang from the backstage pass to send me on outings. One day is still clear to me. Harry told me to meet him at a world-renowned hotel in the area of my town.

I was to go to this hotel with no purse and only the cash I had on me, which was $60. A room would be arranged for me, all paid for by Harry. We were to have a romantic staycation. So, I went off on this adventure, in my delusional state, via taxicab, with nothing except my thoughts guiding me. I had no overnight bag, nothing. Harry had arranged a limousine to take me shopping anywhere I wanted to go. I was thrilled at the thought of this and of finally being able to spend proper time alone with him. I was to get to know him more as a person.

So off I went with my humble taxi driver to the lavish hotel. I arrived and the bell boys opened the door for me and richly escorted me inside. I went to the front desk and told the clerk that I wanted to check into my room. It had been raining for hours prior to this and all I had on was a sleeveless blouse, a pair of capri pants and flip flops. I was so excited knowing that I was going to be treated like a queen. As the clerk looked up Harry's name and information, I waited patiently. Then the clerk reluctantly told me there was no such name in the system and that she knew nothing about this booking. I was mortified! I felt like a large boulder had fallen on top of me. I had been certain that Harry was going to arrive—he said so in my thoughts via telepathy and that was my reality. I could not understand why this was happening to me.

The boulder that crushed my spirits was heart wrenching. I did my best not to cry. I needed a cocktail, so I went to the cocktail lounge where I treated myself to a few glasses of champagne. I had to be careful because I only had my cash and I still needed to pay for a taxi ride home. Then I heard that Harry was still going to arrive at the hotel and that I needed to wait for him. I walked around as he would tell me which spots to meet him. I waited at some of these spots for hours, until a security guard approached me asking me why I was there. He scared me, so I went out of the main part of the hotel and went into the banquet area by the back doors. Harry was to meet me there. I waited until late in the evening. Then I was told to go out in the hotel's park and wait by the fountain. It was raining but I did what I was told. I waited in the cold for at least 30 minutes and then I was told that they were throwing me a party in the ballroom at the hotel next door.

I walked to the adjacent hotel in my soaking wet clothes. I went to the front desk and gave them Harry's name and said simply, "Harry is throwing me a party in the ballroom; can you please direct me to this function." I was excited but angry for all the trouble that this waiting was causing me. The front desk clerk looked at his computer, looked surprised and confused, and said, "There is no function going on here tonight." I could not believe it. I went out the door and hailed a taxi and told the driver that I needed to go home to get my money. I added that from there, I needed him to drive me to the liquor store to get champagne. The lovely taxi driver stated that he would pay for the champagne, and I could pay him back when I arrived at my home. He was a kind man. This was a gift after my terrible day.

The nights were difficult because that is when reality set in. I was scared so I would drink champagne and the Collective Souls would comfort me. Then it would all become too much—I would crash and cry myself to sleep. You must be thinking that I fell off the railcar of the crazy train. I understand what this sounds like, a crazy person doing what the "voices" tell her to do. However, it was not like that for me. I was doing what I thought was real. After knowing what I knew as a spiritual medium and being able to hear spirits whispering messages for their loved ones, it was not difficult for me to believe in telepathy. I can see that muggles might have a difficult time understanding this chapter and why I did what I did. For me it was real. My life had become unleashed. I was living in an altered universe, in a higher state of consciousness, and in a different realm from others. I had attained a level of consciousness that most people meditate their entire lives in order to reach. The only difference was that I was in psychosis, manic and bipolar. I was having a spiritual emergency and I was not aware of it.

Days like this sent me into a tailspin. I continued to believe that I was speaking to Harry via telepathy, and I was angry that I was not able to reach him in real life. All I wanted was to discuss with him what my mind was doing. I recorded more videos about my mediumship experiences and sent them to Harry and the community. I knew something was not right and I wanted help. I asked for help, and it never arrived. I was angry because I had been sent on a wild goose chase and had no answers as to why. In the late evening I looked up Harry on Facebook and saw that he was living a normal life. It was then that sanity filled the room, and I was left standing there all by myself with no Collective Souls. It was lonely and confusing in the moments that I realized that I was not really chatting to Harry. These sane moments did not last long. I would drink champagne to alter my vibration back to the heights I was used to, as I was so high on Spirit.

Chapter Twelve- The Friday Night Lights

Despite walking away from Harry and the other two ministers at the church that day, I still wanted their help. I wanted to discuss my mental health and my mediumship in a non-threatening manner. I had felt threatened when Harry told me I was in psychosis. All that did was scare the hell out of me. The feeling was like being interrogated for a crime I did not commit. I felt misunderstood and not heard. Therefore, I kept trying to get through to Harry by email, which felt safe. I wanted a second chance at discussion but my reach-out failed. I wanted to discuss with him from a psychologist's and professional medium's perspective what was happening to me. I resisted the suggestion of going to the psychiatric hospital, hoping for support from various avenues in my life. Unfortunately, my outreach to other support systems was met with reluctance. Those who knew me distanced themselves, influenced by rumors of me harassing Harry after an unexpected visit to his house. The situation was deeply misunderstood, leaving me feeling isolated and yearning for understanding during this mental health crisis.

Spirit became my new friend and my community. Spirit's whispers were becoming so intense, and I was addicted to them. I wanted only to sit and meditate in a trance state and communicate with Spirit. This is much like other trance-channeling mediums who are popular today, and who channel spirits such as Abraham, Seth, Silver Birch, and others. I meditated for hours every day. I stopped only to get champagne and to eat one meal per day. I ate just enough to keep myself alive. I felt that spirits were my friends, and they made me happy, until I hit the extreme low that would occur at the end of every night.

When I was at my lowest vibration, the Secret Society became abusive. When my vibration was high, the Secret Society failed to exist, and the Collective Souls came in to raise my vibration. I was consumed by this. I lay in bed and daydreamed, and the Secret Society would play tricks on me. I was certainly in psychosis. I could not determine what was real and what was not. That Friday I received virtual messages from Harry wanting to meet me at a nearby mall, and I went there and waited all day for him to show up. He did not show up. It was days like these that sent me spiraling out of control. The day trips full of tricks from the Secret Society were plenty but this day was the worst. I did what this so-called Secret Society wanted me to do, and at night I would crash to an all-time low. That is bipolar with psychosis and mania.

That Friday evening, everything changed in my life. I had just received a letter and a cheque from the church. The letter did not help the extreme low that I was experiencing because I had a strong feeling it was not a good message. I held the piece of paper in my hand and as I started to read it, I felt my emotions plummet to the ground. The Church had told me to stop attending all functions and did not give me a reason why, except to state that I needed medical help and that they were off-limits to me anywhere in the world. As I held the notice, I received a cheque for the deposits that I had made for future classes. It was devastating because they did not give me any empathy or compassion. They did not even try to understand or ask me my side of the story. I had questions—what if I received help, could I have access to them then? Could I go back to courses then? Why were they so afraid of me? What did I do that was so wrong to deserve this treatment? Why was there no compassion for someone with a mental illness?

That same day, Minister Tanis told me in an email that Harry was not available to me and that it would be inappropriate for me to speak to him. All they thought about was the "love" comment I had made to Harry and the fact that I had gone to his house. I had shown up at Harry's house to get help due to wanting to commit suicide. I thought that he could help me. I did not tell Harry I was suicidal that day. I did not have a chance because I walked out on him after he told me I was in psychosis. Harry was a trained professional psychologist and my mediumship teacher. Because of his credentials I had believed he could direct me to the help that I so desperately needed.

I wish my friends and/or family had taken over my business after my crisis, so I could at least have had something to fall back on. I was not in my right mind. I wish Harry had tried to reason with me or, at the very least, had referred me to someone else, as he had alluded to in our previous conversation. I did not push myself on Harry or mention love more than the one time. I had kept my emotions to myself. So the 'love' comment was not a reason to leave me in this crisis. This is especially true after training me to be a medium and working with the mind. This situation deserved more care and attention.

I tried to forget about the letter from Harry and his group. Spirit helped to keep my mind occupied. Spirit came to visit, and I recorded the night on video and sent it to Harry via email. I did this because I thought that maybe he could make sense of it. However, my thought pattern was that the messages I had been sending were not getting through. I thought that my life was hopeless. I was so upset that I could not turn to him for help. The letter sent my emotions into a tailspin. I had no church to go to because I had been banned from it. This last piece of news broke me. I wanted to end my life. Everything seemed so out of control.

My vibration hit a bipolar low point. I crashed completely, and everything seemed lost. I decided to die. I could no longer understand the difference between reality and dream state. I was so out of control. I packed up my vehicle with all my spiritual belongings and all my lifelong mementos to give away to charity. Everything that meant something to me was in the vehicle to be given away. It was the lowest I had felt during my entire life. I felt like everything I had known was a lie. I tried to make sense of it, and I could not. I did not want anything around because I was planning to die. I was determined to complete the task.

It was during that night that I felt like I had died and had never come back to myself. It was the moment that I realized I was alone, with no one to help me on my journey. I was meant to walk this soul road alone. Sometimes in life, events occur that fracture the very foundation on which we stand. Our life, as we have known it, is forever changed, and we find ourselves in an unexpected struggle, first to survive and then to move forward. This was what was happening to me. I was in a struggle to survive. I could not tell the difference between reality and fantasy. I genuinely thought Harry was communicating with me. I thought the dreams I was having were real. Harry was the only person I knew who could help me sort out this mess.

That Friday night I wanted to die—to end my life once and for all. I was determined because I thought my life was a lie. I still believed that someone near and dear to me had raped me and had raped my mom and my sister. I thought that this was real and I had no church community to fall back on, no family and no friends. Prince became my friend, he arrived to see me in spirit and told me he would save me and lead me to the purple rain. The purple rain was the "light", the resurrection in the sky. I drank two bottles of champagne, then took 18 over-the-counter sleeping pills, and fell asleep. I had nightmares about my rape, and it was too much to handle without having anyone to turn to. I told no one about this despair; I simply intended to die. I had lost my entire world, and now I was losing the community that I loved. All seemed lost. It was evident to me that I had nothing to live for.

I felt like the world was against me. I was having nightmares of the rapes, and my mind was confused, thinking it was multiple men gang-raping me. It was definite mania/psychosis. I was oblivious to this mental illness that I had. The only thing that went wrong that night was the fact that I woke up. Surprisingly, I awoke in fear. I was so close to falling back asleep and I knew that if I did, I would die for sure. I fell back asleep, and I was in peace until I heard the voice of my father's spirit tell me to get up, and that I needed to survive. It was then that I saw my parents' and grandparents' spirit, and a feeling overcame me of pure spiritual love.

I was laying there in bed when all these emotions were occurring to me. It was as if I were in hell, and Spirit came through the gates of my hell and pulled me out of the wreckage that I had caused. I felt like I was under a pile of rocks from a terrible storm that had hit me. The wreckage was my body. It felt like a lead weight, heavy, dark, and the feeling of a grenade going off. I was in and out of consciousness, and I recall that Harry was there with me in spirit as well—I was told that he was my gatekeeper. The gatekeeper was to allow me to pass over into the spirit world or stay in a world where hell resides.

I woke up to this feeling of horror, terror, and fear. I was alive, and angry about that, but I was afraid to die at the same time. I could not fully comprehend the situation in which I found myself. I thought Harry, my gatekeeper, was urging me to get up, but my soul was telling me to stay down. Stay down, and it would soon be over, and I could go to God, the Great Spirit whom I knew. Then the gatekeeper stood up and stated that God did not want me to enter yet. My gatekeeper was making me stay on earth longer. I lay back down and knew that this was the end, as my body was shutting down. My lungs were filled with liquid, and my heart felt like it was skipping beats. I was unable to stand and I was unable to talk. The voice in my head told me to lay back down, and I was going to go to God. I lay back down, then I had a fear that I would die. Thoughts ran rapidly through my mind.

I was left all alone in this rubble from the aftermath of my self-destruction. I was scared but I was alive. I could not believe that I had survived. The feeling was like no other. After I was told to wake up, my spirit guides disappeared. It was a scary time for me. I felt like going back to sleep, but I knew that if I did that, I would not survive. Truth be told, I was afraid of the pain because my lungs felt like they were filled with fluid. I decided to live instead. The feeling that came to me after my father's spirit arrived was, "What will I miss if I die?" I then thought, "The pain is overwhelming. It is just too much to bear. I can't come to grips with life. I have cried too much today. I want this not to be true, that it has come to this with me almost dead." I kept losing myself, going in and out of consciousness. My lungs were filling up with fluid, and I felt like I was drowning. It was terrible.

I remember messaging Harry on Facebook messenger to ask for help. I remember what I said to Harry in this message: "God Speed." It is an archaic way of saying goodbye. I then remember calling 911 and then hanging up, wanting to go back to sleep to die. The 911 operator tracked my number and phoned me back. I could barely talk to this operator on the phone, so I forced myself. Now in fear of dying, I tried to stand up, barely being able to, I stood and lost urinary function in my body. I had to hang on to the walls and anything else that would help me stand up. The Friday Night Lights appeared in this posh and quiet town and frightened the neighbors. It was the police coming to the back door of my beautiful home.

Then the ambulance arrived. I remember that the driver treated me with disrespect and had me walk outside to where the gurney was with no assistance. It was terrible, and I struggled greatly. I remember thinking about my life and how I was scared to die. I remember being afraid to lay down on the gurney because my heart was skipping beats. There was no sympathy from anyone around me. When I arrived at the hospital, I received no sympathy, not even from the doctors. It was hell. I believe now that hell is what you put yourself through when you are not in alignment with yourself. I remember feeling scared at the things I would miss if I were to die. It was at the forefront of my emotions. This suicide attempt is something that has changed me. I now understand about life and how precious it is. Life is short; it does not last forever.

I remember the nurses and doctors treating me like I was a drug addict. Asking me question after question. They put me in a room where I was left to suffer until the sleeping pills and the champagne wore off. I remember hallucinating, which led me further down the rabbit hole. My mouth was so dry I thought I was going to die from dehydration. If it weren't for the water bottle I had brought from home, I am sure I would have died. My organs were screaming at me. The doctors wanted to admit me to the hospital to have me see a psychiatrist, but I refused. I told them that I was going to the Church still and that Harry was my minister and psychologist. They then let me go home with no questions asked of me. The hospital let me go home by myself; they told me they were out of taxi vouchers and that I would have to fend for myself.

I went home hours later in a taxi with my slippers, pajamas, and no money. I received no compassion, no empathy from anyone in the world. I remember having the taxi driver wait for me to get payment. I could barely walk to the door of my home. I remember feeling all alone, and that I should have stayed in the hospital. I should have stayed and received the help that had been offered. But when you are mentally ill, you need support from family and friends. I thought I had support but as it turned out I did not. Helping someone who has a mental illness is sometimes difficult. We cannot get through it without help from the people we know and trust.

It was this night that I died and I have never returned to my true self. I told no one about this time until the writing of this book. When I arrived at home, I remember sleeping for only two hours and then going for a long walk because the Secret Society forced me to go out. I was tortured with memories from that night for a long time after. I felt abused by this secret society. It was then that my mother's spirit arrived. I felt her all around me as if she were healing me and trying to bring me inner peace and love. It was the most epic moment of my spiritual life. I sensed Spirit all around, and I was using every sense to feel my mother's spirit. It was as if she had come back from the dead to save me. It felt like her spirit was holding me up. I believe to this day that my mom did come and save me, as did all my relatives in spirit.

I remember not telling anyone in my life about that night except Harry and the community via email and video. I remember meeting with two church congregants shortly after this day, and I believe they were aware of my suicide attempt because I included that in the email. In this cold and brief meeting, they told me that Harry was off limits but that I could go to church but not to the classes. I chose only to hear that Harry was off limits. I was separated from the spiritual advisors and teachers whom I loved, who had helped me turn my life around and had led me to the Great Spirit. I was distraught and destroyed by this turn of events. I thought to myself, what would be the point of attending a church without having access to spiritual advisors who had become my friends? It was soon after this night that the police started to pay me regular visits. The rabbit hole was getting deeper and deeper. As the days went on, I drank more champagne, thereby not giving my body a break from the trauma that I had endured.

The topic of suicide is one that disturbs people. The thought of a loved one choosing to leave this world is disheartening. Suicide is reaching out for some. For me, it was to end my life. The time surrounding this suicide attempt was foggy for me. I can look back now and see what I had done wrong, but back then, I had no idea. It was a cluster of emotions all rolled into chaos. All I remember is the community sending the police to see me yet again, due to the emails I had sent out, crying for help. The police told me to stop sending Harry emails and to end all communication. I had a nervous breakdown. It was an acute stress-induced depression. It was one of the worst times of my life. I realize now how bad the time was. The trauma of my rape memories which came crashing down around me was consuming me. I still believed my life was a lie and I was confused.

Days after my suicide attempt, the police arrived with the mental health authority wanting to take me. I was afraid, as I felt the police were the enemy. They did not approach me with kindness and concern. If Harry had arrived with the police to get me to go to the hospital, I would have agreed to go. People experiencing a mental health crisis require support, which I sought. However, it seemed that all Harry wanted was for me to leave, and he didn't appear genuinely concerned about my mental health. I was able to persuade the police that I was okay.

After my suicide attempt, I was in shock and turmoil. I received a letter from my landlady stating that I was being evicted from my beautiful oceanside suite and that I had two months to evacuate, which is ample time if you are of sound mind. However, I was not in a state to move and to make proper life-changing decisions. I fell deeper into depression, from this bombshell of news. The timing was awful, and I was horrified.

At this same time, I had the tender bid to develop for my seven beauty salons that were up for lease renewal/tender. I had had these contracts as long as I had had the business, so it was a huge deal that they were going up for tender. I would have to bid on them again. It was a large project, and rumors were that there was a large Eastern Canadian company wanting in on my territory. This company had money to work with, and I did not. I paid my staff very well for what they did, and any extra money went to building the business, to my assistant, and for my wages. I was not in the right mental state to compile this tender proposal.

So the Great Spirit brought in, to add to my Collective Soul team, the business tycoon Steve Jobs. I felt the essence of his spirit around me, guiding me, and helping me. His brilliance came through to me, and during this time, I was able to channel amazing ideas with streamlined processes during my mania. Steve helped me with plans to get my beauty company set for the proposal. I also had plans to develop a beauty product line exclusively for seniors. I was set to rebrand my remaining salons, open my business consulting firm, and start to do psychic medium readings via Skype. Steve Job's spirit helped me build several other business brands that I was set to launch in 2018. I was so confident in my business ideas that I emailed business proposals on various subjects to Harry.

Steve Jobs came through. He was a quiet spirit, but his business sense was evident. His vibrations fueled me, and my business sense kicked in. Steve Job's essence and his discarnate (passed) soul helped me to revitalize my business sense and open my mind to this altered state. I came up with alternatives just in case my seven salons would not be renewed. Steve Jobs' spirit helped fuel me during the stress of being manic and running a business.

He helped give me the inspiration to plan, structure, and build two other business model ideas that I wanted to execute.

Steve helped me get my business power back after I found that I had lost seven salons in an outbidding of tender contract to the large company in Eastern Canada. They had won the tender. The six remaining salons were crashing down around me. Nonetheless, Steve Jobs' spirit helped me plan for my future business and to get it quickly set up. I started the business plans, and the websites were all ready to go. However, the mania mixed with psychosis was too intense. The money was scarce, and I needed to plan for this next part of my life since I had been evicted from my home. I needed a budget to keep me afloat. I still thought things would work. I was an eternal optimist when I was in my bipolar highs, and when I was in the lows, it was devastating.

Steve Jobs' spirit gave me the power to get as far as I did after losing the seven salons. However, I was so distracted and manic that I did not arrange to get my supplies transferred over to the other existing salons. The furniture and all my equipment were to be given away. All my assets were simply left behind. During this time, I was focused on my mediumship and my new business. I stepped up the game and developed my two other business models. I did the best I could to maintain things, considering the circumstances. I extended my reach to friends and Harry's community through emails and proposals, anticipating someone would inquire about my situation and offer assistance. However, much later in my journey, I discovered that they had been informed by Harry that I was allegedly attempting to harass him. He cautioned people to avoid me, citing pending legal actions and charges. Rather than receiving the anticipated supportive outreach, my situation took an unexpected turn, escalating into a police case.

I sent numerous emails to Harry, his community, and my spiritual friends, but the responses were quite limited. The male minister from the spiritual church in Alberta was the only one who replied, though it was in a manner that lacked understanding and empathy, suggesting that I should cease contacting them. It was surprising to witness such a stark change in demeanor from someone who was a friend of mine and typically demonstrated compassion and empathy towards me and others.

Turning your back on someone who is mentally ill is a death sentence for them. How I did not try to commit suicide again baffles me to this day. I know now that it was Spirit who saved me from this horrible time. Steve's presence brought in ideas that I built with him in mind. These ideas were terrific. I am an "ideas" person by nature. I love to build businesses. I have done this my entire life. During my manic time, the ideas flowed endlessly. I wish I could be in that state again just to channel more fabulous ideas. Mania can put you in a state where you come up with big dream ideas. My goal at the time was to get my confidence back and have these business ideas in my portfolio and be able to go to an investor who could help me grow some of them. Some of them were global and included housing for the low-to-no income demographic. Food would be prepared for them in exchange for hours of volunteer time, much like a co-op. I called this idea "PurFound". It is a project to help the world. One of the side effects of mania is grandiose ideas. I had lots of big ideas at this time. However, Spirit had a way of getting me to stay grounded long enough to stay alive.

Chapter Thirteen- The Road of Souls

The time grew dark and dreary. The nights were endless. After losing the proposal for seven of my beauty salons and after my suicide attempt, it was evident my vibration was low. I had been a business owner for most of my career. Losing the seven salons sent shock waves through my entire body. I did my best to cope. I did this by communicating with spirit. They were my only friends. The spirits that were brought in matched my vibration at this time. I started to receive messages from murder victims in spirit. The messages were so vivid, and all my senses were activated. These spirit communications were the most profound moments of my life. Spirit showed me the vibrational energy that spirit has when things are dark. I was seeing that everybody gets redeemed somehow and in some way. I call this the "redemption zone" on my mediumship chart. I was realizing things on a different soul level. Spirit showed itself to me in different ways.

The first spirit was a boy who came to be named Jacob. He arrived very vividly because I was using all my senses of mediumship. He wore jeans and a striped t-shirt. He lived on a farm and he was badly beaten up. When he came to me, he smelled overpoweringly of urine. It was my spirit showing me my Clairalience. I felt I was being trained to smell by spirit. Jacob had been beaten and then thrown into a water trough that the horses use to drink water from. Jacob died and this moment was intense for me. I could smell him and his terror. I felt the Great Spirit present when Jacobs's spirit was around. I was being shown my gift to help people in need.

The next unsolved cold case I received from Spirit was a young lady who had been gang-raped and drugged. She had been left for dead with a needle sticking out of her arm. She was wearing black knitted stockings to her thighs, high heeled shoes, a white tank top and a white, shiny, short skirt. She lay in a back alley just off a busy street. She communicated to me that

Spirit took her before she died, so it did not hurt. There was no pain. The Great Spirit was there to take her to heaven. It was such a spiritual moment for me. I cried for her. It was a lesson in faith, trust, and belief in Spirit.

The last person brought to me by Spirit brought back a memory for me. When I was six years old, I went to an elementary school. I walked to and from school daily. One day a large van slowly started to drive beside me. As the side door opened, a man reached out his hand and seemed to want to pull me in. A woman who was in the front passenger's seat went to the back to help the man pull me in. I then saw Spirit, in the form of a young boy, who I did not recognize. He called out to me, "Karen, run!". So I did. Many years later, a little girl Tanya was stolen and murdered while walking home from that same school. In my last nightmare during that tumultuous time, Jacob came to show me Tanya's body as it lay on the ground. She was a little blond girl laying in the dirt. It was an astonishing time for me.

It was a cluster of confusion and stress for me. But even though the time was dark, I was learning lessons that I would never forget. At the time, I thought these spirit communications were cold case files and that I would be working with Harry and the police to solve them. I was told by the Secret Society to post a message on Harry's Facebook page that we would be working with the police to solve these murders. However, Harry retracted my post, stating that it was a fraud. This caused me to become even more depressed and to feel misunderstood.

During this tumultuous time, ideas flowed through me like air to my lungs. Ideas would run rampant throughout my soul, giving me belief that everything might be ok. Nothing made sense at this time. Spirit did not stop at the proposals that I initially sent to Harry. I had amazing ideas that I felt Harry and his community needed to be a part of. I spent hours upon hours of time developing business and marketing plans, creating logos and promotional videos for all the companies that envisioned being a success. I was all set to propose these to Harry and his group of educated professionals. I did not stop there, however. I sent these ideas to some of my friends and to celebrities such as Oprah, Ellen DeGeneres, Tony Robbins, and Abraham Hicks. I printed out the proposals, had them professionally bound, sent them by email and courier to celebrities and to Harry and his community. Unknowingly, it was all a big cry for help. My hope in sending it to the people such as Oprah and Ellen were that I would get on their show after being in contact with Harry. He and I would acknowledge that the telepathy was real, and we could create a stir in the mediumship and spirituality industry worldwide. I thought this telepathy was real and that spirit was evidential. I was a broken woman trying to seek help, but what came across was a deranged person who was mentally ill.

I knew that my mediumship skills were bang on. I was confident, ten-feet tall, bullet proof and in my mind, I knew I was going to be successful. I was also receiving a lot of spiritual communication from the congregants at Harry's church. These congregants were telling me via telepathy that Harry was going to marry me at his church. They had arranged to send someone to my house to do my hair and makeup, and I would get picked up by one of them and be delivered to the church. There was no thought process as to the thought of marrying Harry. I was certainly in a mentally ill state. I remember doing my hair and makeup and it was like the congregants were also with me doing my hair and makeup. I had a round-circle energy healing party and each of these congregants were in my living room. I could feel their souls and their energy.

Afterwards, I would be heartbroken that the night had passed. It was four am and I had missed the wedding ceremony. So, I did what was fun for me—I drank champagne. The champagne kept me from being lonely. I had just me in the world and when I drank champagne it fueled me, so that I was grand beyond proportion. It helped me cope with what I was going through. There were moments of sanity when I would be so confused as to what was happening to me. That was when reality would kick in and I would get so depressed that I wanted to end my life again. I was perplexed by this entire situation. The sane moments however did not last long, only long enough to help me survive.

It seemed like the police were always around; they were haunting me. I was a wanted woman. The police made it clear I would be charged with criminal harassment. They also warned me that if I did not stop emailing, I would have to go to the hospital should they show up at my door again. I felt like the police were the enemy and on Harry's side only. They never asked me at all how I was doing, they only cared about me not contacting Harry. The last police officer who arrived was so intimidating that I decided to move out fast, despite the landlady giving me two months to move. I felt scared for my life, as ironic as that may seem.

I decided to give away the rest of my belongings and get out of town fast where the police could not find me. I continued to unravel. I remember getting rid of my expensive jewelry, and anything else of value that was left. I was eliminating everything that I owned because my intent was to die. I contacted a man to come with a truck and take away all my items for free. All my items were new or barely used. Most of them were brand new because I had lived in the suite for less than seven months and rarely used most of the items. I managed to sell a few items but gave away everything else, even my jewelry. I had one suitcase, lots of pillows, and one blanket left. Once again, I would be homeless. I felt like I was being crucified. It was heart wrenching to see my items go like that. I thought that I didn't have a choice. The police had instilled fear into me. I knew the police would come and lock me away in that horrible place that gave me nightmares- the psychiatric hospital.

I found a place outside of town where no one would find me, at a beautiful bed and breakfast overlooking the ocean. I was to go there the very next morning. I decided to sleep on the floor that last night. It was scary. I had nothing to pack as I only had the bare essentials for living. Mania helped me cope with living because it made me unaware of what was truly happening around me. I lost all contact with everyone, even my staff, and my remaining six salons. I dropped everything; I simply walked away from my life. To this day, I don't know how things played out. I knew money would be running out soon, so I stopped my new business ventures because of a lack of funding and the lack of my faculties.

Spirit kept me alive as my mediumship was flourishing. I was taking everything in stride. I decided to have one last supper in my beautiful home. I chose to make a supper that my two Ukrainian Babas would have been proud of. I felt like I was eating and drinking champagne with spirits. I could hear them laugh as if they were in the same room as me. I was able to see an entirely different world of mediumship than most mediums. It was a world where spirits were enjoying life again through my eyes. I felt my two Ukrainian Babas with my mother right beside me, enjoying the food and champagne. I could hear them chat and laugh as I sat there alone and listened to music. I was Alice, and I was in Wonderland. I was performing physical mediumship, and it was amazing.

When it came time to eat, I felt like I was eating for my mother, and my two Babas. As each spirit came through, I would perform trance mediumship on each one. It was natural and happened spontaneously. I was living for each one of them to have the chance of enjoying one last family dinner together. I had my favorite food, such as perogies and cabbage rolls and champagne—it was majestic. The time was so intense I remember it like it was yesterday. Each spirit came through as their own personality. It was inspiring to know that spirit does not die—it passes over to evolve.

It was so much fun being in this world, and it kept me from crashing in real life. The moments were pure love. It was as if my family were there. It was much like a proper cocktail party that I had prepared just for my spirit friends and me. I heard my Baba laugh as she said to me as I poured myself a glass of champagne- "Well, just a little bit more champagne" in her Ukrainian accent. It was a soul moment with spirit. It is difficult to write about and to do it justice. If I think back to those times, I think that champagne, food, and spirit certainly saved my life. The champagne raised my vibration in the evenings to such a level, it was like drinking water. It was a surreal time for me, and spirit reaped the rewards. We had our last supper together in my oceanside home. I used these coping mechanisms to get by in life as many people do—the only difference was I had spirit to enjoy them with me. My mediumship ability during this time was intense and real. It was as if Spirit came and took hold of me, giving me solace and protection. The time was a magical mystery tour. The magic was from within.

Chapter Fourteen- The Dance

I pull out of the driveway with my vehicle "Walter", and one small suitcase, saying goodbye to my beautiful suite by the ocean. The landlady was glad to see me leave because of the police visits which had become too many to count. I remember the day like it was yesterday. It was a gorgeous, sunny day full of hope and new beginnings. But I was oblivious to the world. My mind was in never-never land, and the road I was about to travel on was paved in yellow bricks. The truth was that my mental health was in crisis, and I did not know at that time what was really going on. I understand now that I was in shock. I believe I was suffering from PTSD, due to the suicide attempt and all the trauma and grief which surrounded it.

I had given away all my worldly belongings, and within a few hours, everything I had worked so hard for was completely gone, with nothing left but memories in my mind. It sent shock waves through my soul when I thought of what I had done. I arrive at the B&B just outside of the city. A lovely lady owned it. It was more expensive than my home near the ocean, but it was far enough from where I had been living that no one would find me. I went there to die. I came to the new place as a broken person. I was a spiritual medium who had fallen down the rabbit hole. I had lost my balance, and everything had come crashing down. It was a bizarre and confusing time. One minute I was happy, the next minute I was not.

The B&B was an oasis for me. It helped me during a time when I was in my darkest hour. I reference this period to a nonsensical time, and I found it impossible to extricate myself from it. Understanding this at the time was impossible. I had left my previous home with only items for survival, nothing else. I was in my leased vehicle which would expire soon, and I had no extra money nor the credit to purchase another vehicle. After 48 years of living, I had nothing to show for it, only myself and one small suitcase. I drove off into the sunset, and I was in denial as to how serious the situation was. It was my Collective Souls and I, travelling this road.

The drive to my new place became exciting. Everything was new to me; life was scary but exciting at the same time. Nothing was familiar. It was chilling for me to realize that my life could change, just like that. The driveway to my new place was long. It seemed as if I were living in a dream. As I pulled into the driveway. I reluctantly walked to the main entry and introduced myself. I was so scared. Then the lovely owner introduced herself. She was very friendly to me and welcomed me with open arms. She walked me to my beautiful suite which had a patio that overlooked the ocean. I had my own kitchen, bedroom and living room. The owner helped me celebrate my move with champagne that I purchased to celebrate the new adventure. I remember her talking so much that I did not need to talk. This was a gift because I had difficulty managing to chat. I was so consumed with mania, psychosis, and possibly PTSD. I had no trouble starting and carrying on a conversation before this trauma, and now, I struggled to find my words.

After we celebrated, the owner kindly left me in my new suite. I could hear the ocean waves from my window. At the time, I didn't want to think about the emotional rollercoaster ride that I was on. I didn't want to talk about it. I steered clear of everyone and everything that reminded me of the horror of a life that I was living. I kept my mind on Spirit and only Spirit. My room at the B&B overlooked the ocean. The body of water consumed me, and that night I wept. It would turn into a daily occurrence. That is the ups and downs of bipolar disorder when untreated. I had come there to die.

Then one night, while Spirit surrounded me like a circle, I lay there in my bed as if I were in a coffin. I felt Spirit start whispering my name and talking to me. I felt my mom, dad, two grandfathers, two Babas, and sister who had passed, all surrounding me. As these spirits formed a circle around my bed, I felt their presence. My father was behind my head, and I felt a heavy weight being put on my body, and my soul lifted like it was a feather. As my soul was being separated from my body, it was evident my loved ones were sending me home to the Great Spirit. They were sending my soul home.

My father spoke to me as if he were whispering very loudly in one ear "We are taking you home, and if you want to live, then I will promise you will marry your soulmate." As he spoke those words to me, my soul felt like it was being ripped away from my body. It was painful. I hesitated. I wanted to go home to the Great Spirit, but I did not want to miss the "dance." I wanted very much to die and go home with my spirits to their vibrational world, but my curiosity as to what was going to be next was tempting me. I wondered, what could be next for me after everything that had gone on before? Would it be possible to marry my soulmate? It was too intense. I decided to stay. The pain was extreme and unbearable. In the next moment, spirit disappeared, and the pain did too.

I was left by myself to ponder this astonishing moment. I will never forget this. That moment changed my life and gave me hope and inspiration. If I did not believe in Spirit before, I sure did now. Spirit came to me that night, and this time it was a completely different feeling. It was a feeling of collection, to take me home to die. It was a very spiritual moment. Death and birth can change a person, I know it changed me. It is moments like this that put one into a completely different space to move forward in life. Spirit was giving me a chance to reflect, adjust frequency, and move on to a completely different viewpoint on life. These are the moments we need to embrace and contemplate.

This spiritual near-death experience that I had was Spirit giving me an "opt out" clause. I chose to stay. I remember Samantha telling me that we are given an "opt out" clause for our life journey to either stay or leave this earth. This is for when we are at death's door and need to decide whether to stay here on earth or exit our physical body. I have never forgotten the moment she told me this theory. I wasn't sure what to believe but after it happened to me, I am a believer. When I decided to stay on this earth just a little while longer, I developed a new outlook on life.

With this new outlook came various spirits to add to my Collective Soul team. These were my "gurus". I was channeling people incarnate such as Tony Robbins, Esther Hicks, Deepak Chopra, Tyler Henry (celebrity clairvoyant), the Dali Lama and others. I would channel what seemed to be an essence of them. I would receive their inspirations to help me survive on a daily basis. I remember seeing Tony, the master expert on television during my teen years, speaking about motivation and empowerment. I ordered his personal power cassette tape series by mail order. He was Tony Robbins. Years after that, Abraham Hicks came onto the scene. This superb lady channeled Abraham, a collection of spiritual teachers who would give her information from Spirit. I remember the time like it was yesterday. These real-life mentors were now my virtual "gurus". Abraham hicks was trying to sort out the vibration of the Secret Society and Tony was trying to motivate me and Harry via telepathy. My mind was very active during this time to say the least.

I now felt the essence of these spirits around me trying to help me survive. I would feel a new sensation come over me, a new essence of spiritual living. Tony's spirit was evident and secure, just like in his movie and television commercials. This was very strong and powerful. He came across as a kind, gentle, person who cared. He felt to me like someone who wanted to help me heal and move on from the torment that I was going through. It was amazing to me at the time, and I felt like it was real. Esther Hicks via Abraham Hicks taught me more about vibration. It was just like when I met her in person years before at retreats. She was now here to sort out my vibration.

These gurus were here to stay, at least for now. Our souls are a vibration. I understand that vibration. How one feels is important in how one's mediumship will work. If my vibration is not high enough on an emotional scale, then my ability to be in tune with the Great Spirit is weaker and not vibrationally in alignment. I have learned a lot from Spirit. I have learned that Spirit also comes in ways of an essence, a softer version of oneself. Some spirits arrive more prominently, while others enter more subtly. It amazes me to this day the different adventures which Spirit brought me. I had definite master class teachers via spirits, both incarnate and discarnate.

The next to come was Nelson Mandela. His was a quick visit that brought me a sense of being at peace with what I had left in my life. Others followed, Dalai Lamas, Buddha, and Paramahansa Yogananda. This team would come in the morning for several months and bring with it love and light. The messages I would get would be of an intense understanding of my Higher Power. I was reminded that all people are on the same journey. I had a feeling of peace, love, and light. The messages were not as strong as my awareness of the spirits' existence. I felt their essence of pure love to heal me, guide me, believe in me, and give me hope. I understood that good things were to come and was reminded to keep in a positive frame of mind. I was told to meditate and to relax my thoughts, to make way for my higher self to emerge. It gave me hope to continue when I was at my very lowest in life.

If it wasn't for Spirit, I would not have survived. The time was so dark and yet so intensely spiritual. I felt the Great Spirit surround me, protecting me from the pain that I had. I drank champagne when my emotions became too intense. Mania would take over my days, and I would go about life like I was on holiday. I would often have nightmares. Differentiating between fantasy and reality was difficult at this time. My undiagnosed bipolar disorder made it impossible to have a balanced outlook on life. The chaos swiftly enveloped everything, casting even hope into disarray. All seemed lost until the night of the dance.

I remember like it was yesterday. The moon and the dark of the night were what captured this moment the most. The dance took place at the B&B in my beautiful suite overlooking the ocean. The view was sent from The Great Spirit. It was mystical, my getaway for three months. Music was playing, a song called "The Dance". It is a song about love with a connection to Spirit. I was enjoying a glass of champagne when Spirit led me to the dance floor of this oceanfront deck. During this time, nothing else mattered, only Spirit. All my Claire senses were heightened, and I felt at peace with what I knew was real.

I would feel spirit's essence around me, the Great Spirit sent me their souls for me to discover. During this time, I was in a trance. As the music played in the background, I heard their spirits' whispers, telling me to hold out my hand. I felt their spirits' touch as they took my soul and encapsulated it. I started to sway, with their hands holding mine. I felt my body float, and Spirit appeared. The song speaks of a dance that is shared with the one they love, beneath the stars above. It talks about how love is never ending. I urge you to listen to the song as you read this chapter. It will bring it to life. The song penetrated my soul as I listened to not just the words, but to how much soul was brought into its creation.

At this time, I felt Harry's soul dance with mine. Other souls also came and had their turn dancing with me. It was like having a party with the people I knew. It was as if Harry was really in the room dancing with me. The moment was not romantic, it was spiritual. It came from God, the Great Spirit that I began to know and my Collective Souls. It was like dancing with someone and making every move as if it were real. To me, it was real. Was Harry my Twin flame? Perhaps. I know for sure it was God bringing us together to learn the hard-core lessons of life and to help us evolve spiritually. The moment was euphoric.

Other souls visited me, incarnate and discarnate. I could distinguish each soul as they entered the room. It was a theurgical, mystical creation that Spirit was showing me. During this time, nothing mattered. Spirit took my hand and led me to the dance floor yet again. The stars were shining, and I was all alone in the world, but not in the universe. I was dancing with Spirit, and it was real. The sound of the ocean was in the background, while Spirit's essence surrounded me. I remember those moments the most. It was just me on the deck, but Spirit came in and took the lead. It was a proper waltz-style dance with dips, twirls, and spins. It was beautiful and inspiring to know that Spirit was real.

The night was mesmerizing. Crossing over to Spirit and spirituality is something that I am passionate about. I am a student of spirituality and mediumship. I am intrigued by this subject and strive to understand more because that night was something that helped fuel my passion for Spirit. The dance was a majestic moment of light and love. I felt multiple spirits in the room with me that night. The dance was so detailed, it made me realize I was waltzing with my father. My father was an amazing dancer, like Fred Astaire. My father was with me that night in spirit, as was my mother. Other spirits were also dancing with me. I could tell the difference as each spirit passed through me. The spirit encounters were real and magnified by mania. I felt Harry's soul communicate with me. I was told by the Collective Souls that our souls were brought together to help each other evolve spiritually.

In the weeks after the soul dance, I started to wonder about soul growth and engrossed myself learning about it. I began to journal about my life, endlessly trying to get to the bottom of what was happening to me and how my life had unfolded. Similar to peeling layers of an onion, my life and memories gradually unfurled, allowing me to comprehend myself on an entirely new level than ever before. I would write hours upon hours each day and send off these journals to Harry at his church. I shared my journals with him to help him understand that I am not a criminal, but a human being deserving of consideration, rather than someone to be dismissed.

SOUL DANCE

When I pondered about the soul dance that night, a memory came to mind as I was writing. It was a memory of spirit coming to visit me. Several times throughout my life, I thought it was my soulmate. Or could it have been my spirit guide or maybe even The Great Spirit? I am not sure, however it felt real. I recognized his presence, his soul, his heart. When he arrived, it was often when I was laying down sleeping, and I would awake with a feeling of someone laying next to me cuddling me. Comforting me. When I was fully aware, I would realize it was not real, it was only spiritual. It actually felt like someone was right next to me and at first, I would get scared thinking someone entered my bedroom—it was that real. But once I was attentive then I would understand it was possibly my soulmate's soul coming to visit me.

When I turned manic, I could not help but feel that this mystical love was Harry. My feelings for the actual Harry were very different. When I saw him, I was very grounded, just like I should be when approaching the minister and psychologist of my congregation. The mystical love part was when I was in psychosis. I brought my two experiences together-the mystical soulmate who was yet to be known and the telepathy stating that he was Harry. I combined it in my mind to create this God of sorts. Was it real? Was it not? I was struggling with this in my mind. I have never been able to explain why it was that Harry was so involved in my life spiritually. It was possibly a case of mistaken soul identity. Harry did not want anything to do with me in real life. So why was I drawn to him spiritually? I believe it was his power of spirit, the Great Spirit that I was drawn to. I looked at his image and saw the Great Spirit instead. I was sure his soul and mine were connected spiritually in some way, possibly in another lifetime. We will never know.

The night of the dance changed my life. I do believe in love and magic all because of spirit. I believe that one's soul lives on, and that spirit is eternal. I believe in the fairy tale because it helps us get through life. I believe that energy is everything, and when you feel good, your energies are in alignment with your higher power of the Great Spirit. I believe that thoughts have power over you. I believe in manifesting. I am a very optimistic person, upbeat, and happy-go-lucky. I believe that when you die, you cross over to spirit, and that your soul will continue to evolve. That spirit can then communicate with the living if they have the power to believe.

The dance with the souls made me reflect on a deep spiritual level like never before. I know for sure Spirit is real. After that night of the dance, I realize the Great Spirit exists in all of us. I know that energy and alignment are real. I know that you manifest and bring into your life what you think about. I know this because the dance was real. I believe that karma is real, that you get back from life what you give out. You are brought into this life with everything you need. Spirit is here to lead the way, to show us what we need out of life. The trick is to clear our minds long enough to listen to the whispers and to feel their gentle touch on our soul. My Collective Souls led the way this night. I started to believe in life again after this soul dance. I started to believe that life was just beginning, and that the best was yet to come.

Chapter Fifteen- Crazy Like a Fox

The phoenix rises, and in mid-flight, it sets fire to itself, to emerge into a new life. I am the phoenix burning in flames. In mythology, a phoenix is a long-lived bird which is born again. Setting fire to itself, a phoenix obtains new life by rising from the ashes. It is associated with the sun. The phoenix creates intense, deathless inspiration. Mystically speaking, I believe Spirit was setting me on fire and giving me an entirely new life. Encapsulated by the souls who surrounded me, Spirit was everywhere, and I saw flames of gold flying high above the ocean air. These flames were in my mind. The moonlight hit the waves. It was mesmerizing. It was my phoenix burning high into the night. I felt my soul touch the earth, and then I was noticed by the Great Spirit. It spoke to me, imparting words of wisdom. I felt God connect with me. The feeling was euphoric. My soul started to burn, and into the ashes, I fell. I was born again.

For the first time in my life, I felt that I could carry on despite everything. It was complete elation. The manic moments were the best. The feeling was fresh with sparkles in the air. It was the feeling that surrounded me—fun, light, and airy. In the days after "the dance" at my refuge, I drank champagne and lived on only one light meal per day. I did not require much food. I slept only a few hours a night. I was living on adrenaline. I remember being scared when I was faced with reality, so I chose to live with spirit and in my mind for the entire duration of my manic getaway. I was oblivious to the life that I had left behind. It had been a rich life, full of people, work, and activity. Now, I was going through the motions, and Spirit would lead the way. Spirit had a firm hold on my soul.

I went to the beach at the bright start of daylight, usually at 6 am. I continued with my day and went shopping, then found my fix by channeling Spirit at night and drinking champagne. My days were very productive. To help you understand my life back then, you must understand the complete interwoven dynamics of my feelings, the side effects, and everything this breakdown entailed. What I want to share with you is that I started to channel advice from spiritual experts on enlightenment. I learned tremendously from Spirit during this time. My senses were heightened beyond belief, and I was under a spell. I was also learning about regular people and how they react during a crisis. I was the empathic psychic medium who lost everything, only to begin again. A hero's journey indeed. I was in the middle of this journey, with my soul arriving to come and save myself. The phoenix rises again after it has been destroyed. I rose again. I rose above the ashes, and I was fighting to regain my breath.

I am a very meticulous person by nature. I am also a very good business person, if it were not for the mental illness that now crippled me. Because of who I was by nature, my team from the Great Spirit was extremely coordinated. Spirit brought in the Collective Souls. This team had mastered the field of spirit—discarnate, and incarnate. Everything else was created by my mind to organize my thoughts and feelings, like the Secret Society which was Harry and his team of mediums. They were mostly cheering for me, but not always. Then there was the Spirit Mafia, who were strictly spiritual, dead souls from the actual mafia, coming to kick the ass of any being of light trying to torture me. Next, there were the Redemption Spirits who were tortured souls. And lastly, there was my new team which I call my gurus. Spirit was the only thing I had left in my life.

I was under a spell. One moment I had been listening to Harry give his sermons, the next I was running from the police. Everything had happened so fast. That is why I went to Harry for help. He was an expert in what I needed help with, which was spiritual mediumship mixed with bipolar, mania, and psychosis. I knew this, yet nothing I did helped me to get him to assist me. I did what I knew was best, I prayed. I prayed hard for what I needed. I prayed to God. I knew everything was gone, and now I needed help. I knew who was arriving next into my world of the Collective Soul—the late and Great Martin Luther King. I was fully entranced with his spirit. His soul was with God and my team of the Collective Souls. I felt his presence. His story became mine. I not only spoke like him, I also became him, if only for a minute. Reverend Dr. Martin Luther King did not stay long, but he stayed long enough to leave me with hope. He told me that people would be called not female or male but "Hues"—short for human. It was his way of saying that everyone would be equal. His presence gave me hope that everything would be ok.

The months went by quickly. I remember the days disappearing entirely, and before I noticed, a week was gone from my life. I felt all alone with no one to talk to but my spirit friends. All seemed lost long before everything went crazy. I felt like I had entered another dimension. Why was I being shown the memories of my rape again? Why did I get the message that my life was a sham? My life was burning in this virtual fire. It was a fire caused by mania and psychosis. I know that my mediumship made things worse for me. Why was I not able to get the attention of the people I needed the most? My life was burning all around me. There would be nothing left to resemble my old life. Fear would set in at night when I was faced with the reality of my so-called life. The soul dance lasted for weeks. Spirit never left, and I would dance obliviously during some of the saddest moments of my life.

Everything I once knew had fallen into this virtual fire and was burning all around me. I was oblivious to what was being destroyed by my actions. At the time, nothing was left from my old life except my soul and my vehicle Walter, and of course, my suitcase. Everything else was gone—my home, my friends, my family, and the community that I had reached out to. Even Walter was not mine, as I needed to send him back to the dealership. I was grieving the loss of my business, where I had worked most of my adult life. I was grieving the loss of my income and my lifestyle. Losing my business was like losing a loved one. It was my everything—it defined me. I stopped paying my personal loan, which caused my credit rating to go down the drain. When I lost my company, I lost my coworkers, who had been my friends for over 20 years. I lost my business associates, and what seemed like my entire career.

I was always in control of my life before, and now I was not. No one in my business life knew what was happening to me. To this day, they think that I just fell off the face of the earth. Not even my former assistant knew where to find me. I remember paying her one last time, and I did not tell her where I was going, and she never asked. This is where the real journey began. I needed to heal. Everyone in the Church community knew that I had had a mental breakdown. I did not want to be found. I wanted to go away to die. I had nothing left that resembled my old life. I believe that someone should have tried harder to help me. I remember going to Martin and Mandy for help and for a place to stay after I received notice of my eviction out of my home, and they refused to help me. They were on Harry's side and chose to stay away from me. Martin clearly stated to me that I had burned all my bridges. That baffles me to this day. The true injustice lies in facing a mental illness crisis without the support of others.

Support was crucial as I grappled with the impact of mental illness, as it was eroding every aspect of my life. In the midst of grappling with the impact of mental illness, my need for support was paramount as it gradually eroded every facet of my life. While a few friends reached out with calls and emails, the extent of outreach was minimal. Surprisingly, it was primarily the Church community that took decisive action, dispatching the police to my aid. However, the presence of the police, while well-intentioned, proved to be threatening to my fragile state. What I truly needed was the support of love and kindness, rather than people who, perhaps out of fear, were not equipped to address the complexities of mental illness. The disparity in responses underscored the urgency for more comprehensive assistance during such a crisis, as simple gestures over the phone fell short of addressing the depth of my needs.

I was managing to claw my way out of that situation and everything else I have been through with no help at all. I remember watching a movie called The Cobbler, with actor Adam Sandler. It is a movie about understanding life through the other person's perspective. It showed me that we must be kind to one another. I want people to realize that even if someone looked fine, they may be hurting. Be compassionate with each other. Try to understand each other on a deeper level and know that sometimes people do not always ask when they need a helping hand. I was mentally ill, and people were afraid to approach me, so they sent the police instead. This led to my wreckage. Everything was lost when I took the soul dance. What I did not know was that a new life had yet to begin.

The days of living by the ocean were some of the best days of my life. They were also some of the worst days of my life. I spent the Spring and part of the Summer at this lovely oasis. It was June of 2017, and I was having the time of my life for the most part. Mania will do that. I went with the owner of the B&B to the bar, to commemorate my father's passing on Father's Day. As we celebrated, we discussed my fond memories of my father. When we arrived back at the B&B, a police vehicle was in the driveway. They had found me because in the last email I sent to Harry, I had mentioned where I was. This was my fault and a manic accident. Or was it fate? The police officer was gentle and kind towards me, especially when I told him of my father passing on Father's Day. He simply told me to stop communicating with Harry and the police wanted to interview me when I was ready. It was nonthreatening, unlike the police had been prior to this in my suite by the ocean.

Days later, I went for the interview, because the police officer was kind, and I felt safe. Before the interview started, the officer stated to me that I could leave at any time I wanted and that it would be recorded. We chatted for about 30 minutes, as I tried to explain to him that I only wanted to chat with Harry because he would understand what I was going through, with being a medium and all. The police officer then changed his demeanor and asked about the "love" comment I had made to Harry. He was trying to get me to talk about my so-called obsession with Harry. The officer informed me that Harry was married, which was a surprise to me. I did not care either way because it was only spiritual love that I felt for this minister and teacher. I knew that I was not a love-crazed stalker. In my reaching out I was only stating that I wanted mediumship help.

I was confident within myself. Looking back, I can now understand that I felt a connection to Harry because he felt safe to me, and he was different from any other man that I knew. I started to understand that I was not getting through to this officer. So I started to walk out. The officer seemed surprised and asked me where I was going. I told him, "You told me I could leave at any time." He let me go. As I was leaving he told me to call my family. I replied that I would not call them. To this day, I do not know the full extent of what the police were told by Harry, his community, and my family. As I walked away, I felt ten-feet tall and bulletproof.

I knew my days at the B&B were running short. I needed to make a move and needed to do so fast. Money was running out as I had no income coming in, and I was spending money quickly. That is a manic trait. In fear of the police coming back to get me for good this time, I moved to a less expensive place near a lake. It was in a beautiful new condo with a flatmate named Frank. It would be a stretch for me because I had never had a roommate, but I had no choice. I moved into a ridiculously small room. I purchased a twin-size bed and called it home. Frank was in his late 20's. He was seldom home. I did not think Frank was the type who understood about mediumship and spirit. I told him that I was a vocal coach, and that I was training via Skype for a theatrical production in England. Therefore, if he heard voices, he would know that I was working. I thought I was clever. It worked. He was impressed. I had fun during this time but kept inside for the entire summer and part of the fall. I went out only to get champagne. There was a casino within walking distance, but I did not go there. Gambling was the furthest thing from my mind given that I had the entire spiritual realm to entertain me.

I continued to work on my mediumship chart for my mediumship vibration zones which would impress anyone interested in this spiritual trade. I planned to teach the lessons that I was learning from my Collective Souls. I had a blast by myself but the truth of the matter was that I was living a sad existence. I started to worry about money. I calculated that I would have enough money to live on until the following year in March. Then I would be penniless. For the most part I thought I would just die. It was not hard to believe. I thought I would snap again and be successful at killing myself.

Summer flew by, and Fall began. It was a very lonely time with just me and Spirit. The day that life changed for me was the day I started to channel the famous Fox sisters named Kate and Maggie—I knew them as the Spiritual Fox Sisters. They were mediums from the year 1848. Their spirits arrived, and they were members of the Collective Souls. The vibration throughout this day was positive. I remember being so excited. I designed a book cover for the book I would write with Harry via telepathy, on the famous Fox sisters. I was going to name the book, Crazy Like a Fox. It was a great start to the day. I had no champagne and not much food that day. Then as darkness crept up on me, I cracked. The voices of the Spirit Mafia and the Secret Society started and became too much. The voices were starting to become abusive.

So, in October 2017, I posted on social media that I was going to kill myself. I had lost it completely and posted on Facebook that Harry was mind raping me, which I thought he was. The police showed up at my door hours later. They found me via my computer address. When the police arrived, I was in my pajamas. They did not let me change. Three vehicles showed up—one police vehicle, one ghost car, and one regular vehicle which the mental health authority person drove. The officer knew everything about me, and he tried to reassure me that everything would be ok, and he said that I would start to feel better soon. He told me I was in a position called "failure to thrive." This is a term used when someone cannot cope with their life and/or the environment. I felt relieved.

I took nothing but my purse. As it turned out, they were planning to keep me for a long time. Frank was the one who answered the door. He seemed astonished. As the police escorted me out of the apartment, I simply told him that I was not feeling very well and that I had to go. I wanted to die, but Spirit was keeping me alive against my will. I was planning to go to the Victim Services Department at the police station later that week because I was running out of money and was not capable of survival. Instead, the police had found me. As we drove to the hospital, the police officer who was not in uniform began to talk to me like we were old friends. He had read everything that I had sent to Harry. He knew my entire story: about my two dogs who had died, about all the turmoil, loss, and grief that I was going through and he gave me compassion. I will never forget that moment. During my most challenging times, I sought compassion from Harry and his community, but unfortunately, all I encountered was a lack of support.

We pulled up to the hospital, and the undercover officers, the uniformed police, and the mental health authority person and I walked in as a team. I wanted my spiritual team. As it turned out, this would be my new team. I had arrived at the place where Harry wanted me to go, which was the psychiatric hospital. And just as I had feared, nurse "Kravitz" gave me a pill cup with medication in it—no questions asked. I had not taken medication nor drugs of any kind before. I refused to take it, and the nurse stated that I had to take the medication, or I would be restrained and forced to take it. I obliged and took the medication. All my rights were stripped from me. I was now in the hands of the mental health authority. They make the decisions regarding your health and wellbeing. It was frightening.

The waiting room was where we slept at night. All the guests were removed, and the patients were expected to sleep on the waiting room chairs which had been pulled out in the same room. It was what I had to do for two full nights and two full days. You go through the motions and do what you must do to get over the situation. It was terrible having no one to call, and then I was forced to contact my family. I felt humiliated. With little discussion as to how I was doing, I was told by the doctor that I was manic and that I had bipolar. They put me on three different types of medication. During this time, it was like I was in jail. The nurses treat you like your voice does not matter. The first day was very scary. I spent almost two months in this mental health hospital.

Finally I was admitted into the hospital and out of the waiting room. I remember a nurse coming to my door to take me for electric shock therapy otherwise known as Electroconvulsive therapy (ECT). She said, "you are Karen?" I said "yes, I am Karen." They were there to take me away to get me zapped. I refused, so when the nurse double checked my file, they realized that they had the wrong Karen. I was so relieved. I was so frightened that I would have to have the electric shock therapy just like in the movie One Flew Over the Cuckoo's Nest.

Once the medication kicks in, being hospitalized is not glamorous. You are exposed to all kinds of people with varying degrees of illness. You are expected to follow the schedule, to eat, and to participate. I stayed almost two months in the hospital, and during the entire time I had only one friend visit me from my spiritual community. Her visit meant a lot to me. The time was sad and lonely. I was fighting like hell to get back to myself. If I had had a physical illness, I would have had visits from family, friends, and from my spiritual community. But it was a mental illness so no flowers, and only one visitor.

I was assigned to a social worker, a mental health worker, and a psychiatrist. The social worker I was assigned to fought hard for me to get myself together. She contacted my family to see if they could support me financially or in any other way. The support that I was offered by my family was my nephew Dustin offering for me to stay with him until I got on my feet again. This touched my heart, as Dustin and I were always very close until mental illness creeped into my life. Dustin lived in Alberta where I had lived. I was too stubborn to move back there, a broken woman. I graciously declined the offer. I was on my own. My flatmate Frank wanted me out.

Once again, I was homeless. The hospital was threatening to release me into a homeless shelter. The prospect of being released into a homeless shelter loomed ominously, sending shivers down my spine. The sheer thought of facing such a dire circumstance filled me with an overwhelming fear that reverberated through every fiber of my being. The uncertainty and vulnerability associated with homelessness intensified my anxiety, amplifying the distress I was already grappling with in that challenging moment. The hospital agreed to let me off on day passes to look for a place to live.

While I was out on a day pass, I found a rooming house to rent for $450 per month which housed five other people. It came furnished and was just down the road from the B&B. That is a far cry from the million-dollar mansion that I was accustomed to living in just several months prior. The thought of moving there made me cry. My social worker set me up with welfare. I started at $740 per month, then months later I would be advanced to disability pay. I would then receive $1132.00 per month. It was scary for me. I was used to spending that kind of money in a week. It was a major life shift.

When I arrived back to the hospital from my day pass, I found out that Harry and the Church were pressing charges against me for criminal harassment. It was due to all the emails and videos which I had sent. When I heard that news, my soul shivered in pain. I felt betrayed, that moment forever changed me as a human being. I lost all hope and faith in people and their trust.

I did my best to forget about the situation and I started to indulge in the lovely hospital food they had prepared for me. That night, my dinner arrived on time, much like on a cruise ship. I had chicken breast with mushroom sauce, rice with butternut squash, and broccoli. My chef salad and minestrone soup for appetizers were to perfection. The yellow garment they had me wear was like a straitjacket minus the ties. Very uncomfortable. You must wear their garments at first, then you can earn the right to wear regular clothes. You also require special privileges to go out to the garden area and to go outside. This, too, is like that luxury cruise resort where if you pay extra, you get more privileges. My room number was number 128. It is a room that will one day be famous. "The famous author Karen Rose Kobylka wrote her entire book here while in a manic state." That was my goal back then. I would spend as much time as I could writing in my room about my journey. My mind became clearer, and the Secret Society and the Spirit Mafia were gone. Spirit was also disappearing. This fact made rethink the entire spiritual world that I had believed in. My life has been torn down to nothing.

What served as a profound revelation for me was the stark reality that only one person took the time to visit me during my hospital stay. She was a friend from the Church, with whom I wasn't particularly close, and who had faced challenges within the Church community. Her act of compassion in coming to see me stood out amidst the absence of those closest to me. This poignant moment marked a turning point where my faith in the world waned.

As days seamlessly turned into weeks and then months, I found myself adapting to the solitude that had become my new normal. The unsettling truth was that I hesitated to move forward, gripped by the fear that I lacked a support network – facing the world with limited connections and a profound sense of isolation.

Chapter Sixteen- Jail Time

The psychiatric hospital had become a safe haven for me. I remember my last day in the hospital. I was not ready to leave. My mind felt muddy from the drugs they had forced upon me, and I shook constantly as a result of them. My body was simply not used to those foreign substances—only champagne for this girl (those days are long gone). As I packed the plastic hospital bag of all my worldly belongings, I wondered what court would be like. It was where I was sent to after being discharged. I was being charged with criminal harassment by Harry and my Church community. I reluctantly said my goodbyes to the nursing staff and the few friends that I had made in the mental hospital, and I drove away in my expired, leased and "souped up" Ford Escape "Walter". I remember wondering if the Bailiff who threatened to take my vehicle away months prior would be able to find me where I was headed.

I was ordered by the courts to go immediately to the courthouse upon leaving the hospital. As Walter and I pulled up to the courthouse, I reached into my designer purse and dug out what little money I had to pay for parking. I remember walking inside and having the urge to cry. I fought back the tears and wondered how it was that I had lost everyone and everything in the world that was dear to me, either through death or through this disastrous situation. I bit my lip hard, so I would not cry. I arrived at the check-in station. They asked me my name. I told them. It was declared earlier by my social worker that I would get special attention because I was a patient in the hospital. My social worker reported that they would be kind to me. I waited quietly for my escorts to bring me to the courtroom when two sheriffs arrive in uniform and with guns in their holsters.

They read me my rights and put hand and foot cuffs on me as if I were a hard-core criminal. It was not exactly the special treatment that I had in mind. I immediately went numb and no longer felt like crying. I am sure I was in shock of some kind. We walked down the long concrete hallway with stark florescent lighting until we reached the jail cell. It was a concrete room, painted beige with graffiti engraved in. There was only me in this cell, which contained a toilet and water fountain combo unit for my convenience. Yuk! I sat on a steel bench and was told that it should not be longer than 30 minutes until the judge called for me.

I remember waiting for just over two hours until the sheriffs came to get me for court. During this waiting period I reflected...how did I get in this situation? I had arrived in this new oceanfront city, my vision board intact, wanting a new lease on life. I had hopes of growing my chain of 16 beauty salons to 30 and now they were all gone in a New York minute. How is it that a Law of Attraction junkie can get this low in her life? Where did it all go wrong? Spirit assures me that I am in the right spot but how is that so? What led to such a disastrous turn of events? How is it that I am running a beauty empire by day and performing platform spiritual mediumship on stage by night one moment, and the next I am mentally ill and homeless?

As I waited in the cold jail cell, I pondered about my life in this half-trance, half-comatose state. How did I get here, on this island of hope turned terror? I remembered my time as a little girl filled with faith and inspirations that life would be like that Cinderella story I had loved as a child. I reflected as I awaited sentencing and thinking about how my life turned out. The two hours that I had to wait in jail seemed to last forever as a song played in my head by the Dixie Chicks, "I'm not ready to make nice." How did I get to this situation where I am all alone in life? I was being treated like a criminal. It was enough to want to end my life again, yet I was not allowed to die. The time was dark, and there was not a friendly face to be seen. Two sheriffs came to take me to the courthouse. I arrived in the courthouse without cuffs. It was a time that stripped me of everything I once knew about myself. My self-confidence was destroyed.

The jail was interesting. I felt like I was living a nightmare. I did not blend well with this criminal environment. The sheriffs directed me to a bench just outside of the courtroom. The lawyers milled around asking who had representation. I said I did not, so I was given a court appointed lawyer. This lawyer asked me my situation and reviewed my file. We then walked into the courtroom. He seemed to know what to do. I tried not to cry. The judge was not one to mess around with. Everything was very serious. I was sentenced to probation twice a month. Probation consisted of going by bus to the city to sign in with a probation officer. I was to stay away from Harry, and his spiritual community. I was prohibited from contacting him on social media and any other form of contact. I was to go to court again for final sentencing later on. Soon after, another lawyer was assigned to me, and I was to go visit my probation officer once a month. I was also to get a psychiatric assessment later that month.

I planned to go for a drink after court at the local pub so I could conjure up some liquid courage to move into this place. The people in this pub were friendly, but the atmosphere was rough, similar to the bar in the movie "The Roadhouse" with Patrick Swayze. When I arrived there, I kept to myself. I went in, and for the first time in over two months, I had a drink. I had two glasses of white wine. It was a coping mechanism to get me to calm down so that I could adjust to this frightening new situation. I then went to my new home. I was scared and lonely and did not have a television. I had nothing except my soul. I had the time to think, relax, and unwind. There would be no more champagne nights for me. Also, food was scarce and I had my appetite back from the medication that I was being forced to take.

The boarding house was not up to the standards that I was used to. The people there argued with each other, which made the living situation uncomfortable. The kitchen was dirty and busy most of the time. I found this difficult. There was no living room to share, and the kitchen table was used for storage. It made eating very hard. I was confined to a small bedroom. I had brought my own bedding, which made things a little comfier. I had to learn to adjust to new living situation. I would soon be stripped of my vehicle. In the days leading up to taking it into the dealership, I started to develop anxiety. These feelings were new to me. Anxiety consumes your entire being, and you worry for the sake of worrying. I was experiencing Generalized Anxiety Disorder and it made life difficult.

What I endeavored to focus on was the positive, but it often proved challenging without a support system. During this crisis, a time when family and friends could have come together, I found myself grappling with isolation. Instead of rallying around me, people, including those closest to me, offered only sporadic phone calls. As a result of mental illness, I lost my main sources of contact in this world, and the life I had diligently built crumbled without anyone stepping forward to help me pick up the pieces. Despite my efforts to showcase resilience, the absence of a supportive community left me feeling profoundly alone. The world I once knew came to an end, and even the picturesque view from my new rooming house, overlooking the ocean with beautiful walking trails nearby, instilled more fear than comfort. This new chapter, marked by roommates in close proximity, was a stark departure from the solitude I was accustomed to.

The nightmares were gone, and so were my Collective Souls. I had never felt so abandoned by Spirit and the people in my life. It was a plain hard cold truth that I was alone. The blurred memories of my life became clear, and it was evident that I was raped solely by Paul and never by someone near and dear to me. It had been my psychosis playing tricks on me. I was slowly starting to heal my mind and there was the deep realization that my life was completely different than it was before. I had no choice but to get used to this new life. I checked out the bus schedule to find out that the bus only ran only on weekdays four times per day because of where I lived. It would make it exceedingly difficult to get around.

All of this was a huge eye-opener for me as I was used to getting what I needed with the simple snap of my finger. Previously I had the income to buy whatever I needed. I was an idea person, and I simply built another business if I needed more money. Now I needed to heal and recover from my mental illness, and I was not capable of dealing with business during that time. I was also used to long vacations. I had gone on two-week cruises with Samuel, and we vacationed in England, Guatemala, Nicaragua, the Caribbean, and all over North America. I had paid my way for every vacation I had taken. It was something that I was proud of. When I was with Samuel, I paid my share of the bills and "then some." Now I could barely afford to live or eat, and there was no money left at the end of the month for extras of any kind. I did not feel I was strong enough emotionally to work. This entire situation shook me to the core of my being.

I felt stripped of any confidence, dignity, and self-respect. I became emotional very easily. Nonetheless, I settled into my new home the best I could. I started to get my regular appetite back which was not good timing because money was scarce. I found a comfortable coffee shop to write at, just a short bus trip away. I treated myself to a coffee and muffin daily and started to write this book. As I wrote, the words flew off the pen. I went to the coffee shop every day to get myself out of the house and to raise my vibration. I wanted to be with people, even though they were not my friends. It made me feel like I was not as alone as I was. It seemed that everything was more difficult. I was not allowed to leave the area I was in because of my probation.

Understanding my life and where I have been, I have seen the darkness, and through all the pain, sorrow, tears, and debilitating change, I have finally come to a new awareness of myself. I struggle with the depression that, at times, consumes me. I have learned to fight my way through the despair. I now realize that the person who was present during my year-long breakdown was not me. It was instead a lost part of me which mania took over. I can now understand that when someone is manic, they do things out of the ordinary. What I was now experiencing—sadness, frustration etc., were the emotions that I had previously pushed down.

I have learned to forgive myself for the challenges that arose, understanding that my struggle with mental health was akin to someone grappling with a physical illness. People in my spiritual community, unfortunately, misunderstood my journey. My hope is that by sharing insights into this disorder, our community can unite with peace and understanding. More importantly, I seek forgiveness, recognizing that the misunderstanding may have caused pain. Understanding that forgiveness is a part of their individual journey, not mine, I acknowledge my responsibility for the impact of my actions. Through this process, I have gained a deeper understanding of my own journey.

To me, judging a person without hearing the complete story is terrible. This is especially true when it is out-of-ordinary behavior. I feel that society is only at the beginning stage of understanding mental illness. Knowing this, I strive to help people understand that it is a disorder and that it does not define those who have it. It is separate from us. Awareness can be brought to the forefront so that mental health is understood with compassion and understanding. Every person has a story, and with compassion for that story comes a greater understanding of mental health.

While I was living in this rooming house, I did not go to see the ocean because I was too depressed. Depression is a serious illness which many people face. It is a struggle to do the little everyday tasks such as showering and self-care. Depression consumes you, and you are held captive inside this mental illness. I was faced with my emotions for the first time in my life. There were no coping mechanisms to be found. There was only me and these emotions. The days were lonely without any champagne, food that I loved, friends, Spirit, or television to keep me occupied. However, I made the best with what I had. Later that month, I managed to buy a television with the little money I had left. It would be my heirloom. It was purchased at Walmart and cost less than $300. It was a far cry from the last television I purchased (my 65-inch smart television with surround sound) that I kindly gave to my oldest sister upon leaving Alberta.

Times were different, and I was mourning my old way of life, and the old me. I didn't recognize who I was. Spirit was gone, or so I thought. I was used to channeling Spirit through my trance channeling. I could not do that in my rooming house. I did not want to. I had changed after being in jail for the short time I was there. Being charged with criminal harassment made me severely depressed. Something had shifted in me. The old Karen was gone, and I had yet to find the new one. All I ever really wanted was to be saved from this mental illness. When I went for help, I found an enemy instead. This was truly something that I needed to recover from.

Being in recovery from a mental illness, I had a lot of time to think. I used this time wisely. I went regularly to the local coffee shop and I wrote. Christine, the manager, and Alex, the assistant manager, and their staff Julie, among others, were gracious to me as I would spend hours upon hours there writing my heart out. I found solace in this beautiful, friendly coffee place which many others frequented. I was becoming a familiar face. I was introduced to new friends, one of whom was Vivienne. I met her on a desperate day. On my meager budget, I had decided that I needed a psychic reading. Vivienne did tarot healing readings at the coffee house every Tuesday from 2 -5:30 pm. I approached Vivienne and paid her the modest $25.00 she charged.

What I eventually found in Vivienne was a friend, a friend turned family who I could count on. My finding Vivienne was a gift from the Great Spirit.

Her husband, Brian, is also a gem. When I saw them, they quickly fell into my heart center, and I fell in love. This was an honest love which held no threats. It was so pure and gentle that I thought, my God, this is truly a gift from the Great Spirit. Vivienne and Brian's friendship helped me from not killing myself. I still felt very alone, but they helped cushion me from the blow.

I had been accustomed to being alone, but not this alone. My former circle of friends then distanced themselves from me, excluding me from their community and blocking me on social media. A significant portion of my soul sisters treated me as if I were an outcast. It's a unique kind of loneliness when people you were once close to want nothing to do with you. It appeared that everyone sided with Harry. It was something that crushed my heart, realizing that I would be all alone on this soul journey. It was this situation that made my depression even worse. I lost faith in people and society. It became difficult to communicate with people because of this. I had lost all hope.

I was slowly being reintroduced to myself once the medication kicked in. I guess they call it finding yourself. I tried hard to discover the underlying reason that I had developed bipolar. I believe that everything is based on vibration and the emotions that we feel. Through writing, I discovered all about Karen. I was doing my best to survive in this terrifying new world that I found myself living in. I was asking myself, what was Spirit and what was not? I was still able to channel, but it was confusing to me as to what was real and what was not. I had lost my faith in Spirit, and I was trying to gain my faith back. I had slowed down my communication with Spirit to almost a halt. I was afraid of losing all my spirituality. I was confused about Spirit and how it was choosing to communicate with me. The daunting task of comprehending my new way of life and spirituality became too heavy to carry, leading to a gradual erosion of my faith in life.

Through writing, I started to understand my journey on a deeper level. I realized that there is a very fine line between insanity and mediumship. When you are insane you have delusions and hallucinations. When you are a medium you can hear and see spirit. What is the difference? One is a mental illness the other is not. A very fine line indeed. What do we make up, and what do we hear from Spirit? I felt stressed by this gift which the Great Spirit had bestowed upon me and I had questions. For example, how do I use this gift to help people? How will this medication affect my mediumship abilities? When I took the time to channel Spirit, it was only slightly there. I was afraid it was gone forever due to the medication. The voices and the confusion were gone. I felt abandoned by the Collective Souls and I felt as if my soul was in the darkness of despair.

In my despair, barred from attending any spiritual church, I sought solace in alternative forms of spirituality, delving into the teachings of the Tao Te Ching. This is a Chinese philosophy and is the name of a book by Lao Tzu which means "old master". Lao Tzu was a wise man. The book dates back to the 6th century BC. The title translates very roughly to "The Way of Integrity." It contains 81 verses on how to live in the world with integrity. I poured myself into this spiritual way of life, as well as into the Law of Attraction. I spent hours every day and night on YouTube, watching videos on how to find enlightenment and how to raise my vibration. I found serenity in the Tao Te Ching. It gave me peace when I needed it. It gave me a reason to live when I wanted to die. It gave me hope when there was none. It made me realize that when you are broken, you are on the right track because you understand what it is like to be broken. When you are finally healed from what ails you, you can recognize that. It made me feel that all was not lost. Without the sadness, I would not have known happiness.

The truth was that I was clinically depressed. I was on one medication called Abilify. It may have been an easier journey had I asked to be put on antidepressants, but I do not like medication at all. I suffered through the best I could. I was trying to survive in a world where there was very little money and very few resources available to me. I wanted to go to counselling, but you need to be able to pay for this service. Even low-income people need to pay a minimal fee. I could not even afford this. This is barbaric to me considering people who are impoverished need it the most. This makes it difficult to shift out of a depressive state of mind. I was consumed with how to find closure in this situation.

Court was coming up for me, and in the meantime, I was to sign in once a month to the probation office like a real criminal. Things were desperate for me. How I managed to get up and go to the coffee shop daily baffles me to this day. I needed to see my new social worker on a monthly basis also. This new social worker did not seem to like me, which made my journey of recovery even more difficult. However, I was forced to follow this protocol because I was under the mental health authority court order.

Chapter Seventeen- The Injustice System

In the distance there is a light. I see this light because I understand the darkness. I am left with nothing but myself, who I am no longer familiar with. When you are broken into a million pieces, you soon realize that life is not what it seems. I was a broken woman and fell into a million pieces, and I could not be put back together in the same way. Much like in the nursery rhyme, Humpty Dumpty, that is how I felt. It had not been long since the turmoil had begun, and yet I felt like it had been a lifetime of torment. I spent the winter months writing and trying not to worry about where I was going to get my next meal from—I was that poor. I am still suffering repercussions from the lack of food that I experienced. It was frightening. I had to dig deep to understand what was happening to me. I was clinically depressed because of several different dynamics. One was my bipolar and the other was that I had been charged with criminal harassment by my community. In addition, I had lost everything I once knew.

I had no one to talk to about the demons that lay within me, and on my budget, I could not afford to go to a counsellor. It is a barbaric thought that the people who need it the most are not able to go seek help. I also thought to myself, how would a counsellor deal with my situation? The closest person I had in my life who would understand my situation was Vivienne. I told Vivienne about how I felt Harry was my twin flame and how I could communicate with him. I needed to tell someone. It was killing me to be so alone and not tell anyone about my journey. Vivienne was gracious and shared her stories of spirit communication with me. Together, Vivienne and I realized that Harry was most likely my twin flame. Our souls were brought together to help each other learn and evolve. It was not romantic at all, it was the universe helping me evolve past the trauma I had endured.

I also had other things to worry about, such as being without a vehicle. I had been driving as young as 13 years old out in the country. I had always been with a vehicle. My father had provided me with a vehicle until I was old enough to purchase one for myself. So the day that "Walter" my beautiful vehicle was to be returned to the car dealership, Vivienne and her husband, Brian, drove me back home after. It was a blessing to have them with me. I began to understand that I was much like my father, strong and persistent through the tragedies of life. Walter was gone but I took this better than I thought I would. I took the bus to go to the coffee shop during the week as it only ran during that time.

On the weekends I continued to write so that I could discover the core dynamics of why it had all happened. I engrossed myself in writing poetry and studying the Tao Te Ching. Vivienne and Brian introduced me to a motivational nutrition company which helped me get back on track in terms of my health. We partook in events periodically and this was the only enjoyment in my life back then. Vivienne gave me hope that my life was going to improve. She is like I once was, enthusiastic, bubbly and an eternal optimist. For myself, I did not recognize who I was anymore. I rarely smiled or laughed, and if I did, it was fake. I felt sad all the time, and when I woke in the morning, all I wanted to do was sleep and die. The situation was critical for me. I had yet to find my groove. I loved the sparks that flew off Vivienne's auric field. I, on the other hand, was the walking dead. How does one get their life back after such an experience?

Winter went by, and my sisters pitched in for a plane ticket to Alberta for Christmas of December 2017. When I went there, it was depressing. I could not recognize who I was anymore. I could not pinpoint what was happening to me at the time, but I was not myself at all. I remember seeing my brother on Christmas Eve. I just cried, and he gave me a long hug. I saw my nephew Dustin. When I saw him, he told me the offer to let me move into his place was still available. However, it would have meant a long distance move and I felt like I did not belong in that city anymore. I moved to the Island of Hope with a purpose – to embark on a new life. I was determined not to let challenges overcome me because, after all, my mother gave birth to a warrior, not someone who gives up.

SOUL DANCE

I arrived home just before New Year's Eve 2017. I came back to my boarding house and bought champagne to celebrate. It was just me in my small and quaint room. I was very sad and very lonely. I made the best with what I had. I spent the next year working through my emotions by writing poetry and more writing. I have been working on this book since October of 2017. It was through writing that I met some of the most amazing people. People in the coffee shop were slowly starting to notice me as a regular and started to chat with me more. I was introduced to several people who I call my friends today. One is a fellow named Gary. Gary is a kind soul and lives alone in a cabin and is the epitome of a living spirit. He lives a peaceful life, something I know we could all learn from. Gary has taught me a lot about how to continue with life on just the essentials and how to be happy doing so.

Vivienne introduced me to a lovely lady named Linda. Linda befriended me when I had no one except Vivienne as a friend. Linda and I went on day trips by bus to explore what the world was gifting us—the pure beauty of the unknown. Neither of us had a lot of money, but we had each other, and we explored the area as if we were rich. It brought pleasure to my life when I needed it the most. I found pleasure in the little things. Linda, much like Vivienne, is a kind soul, peaceful by nature and lovely. They are both what I needed because I had trouble smiling and being happy. Their friendship was certainly a gift from the Great Spirit.

At the coffee shop, I would see the regulars daily, and I would see this beautiful lady, who would saunter in by herself and sit in the comfortable chairs and drink her latte. I would sit at the table so that I could write comfortably. After months of seeing this same lady, she eventually wandered in my direction and introduced herself as Amy. Amy is a peaceful lady who is quiet by nature and friendly. She is calm and tranquil. I can best describe her by saying that her soul is at peace. Her vibration is such that she is connected to who she is at a soul level. I could tell that she too has had turmoil in her life, and she has learned to deal with this and has been on a similar road to enlightenment as I was. Months passed, and I soon began to know Amy on a friendship level that can best be described as my bestie.

I was slowly meeting people, but I could still not shift away from the sadness that lay within my soul. I still could not recognize who I was. I was once a bubbly, upbeat extrovert who would meet people at the drop of a hat. People used to gravitate to me, and I would be friendly and outgoing. Now I was the opposite. I would be going to court soon, and that depressed me. The court date kept being postponed month after month. I was consumed with grief, knowing that I would need to go to court and have to sign into a probation officer. My entire year of 2018 became consumed by these worries. The outcome would determine whether I was to have a criminal record.

Winter passed, and Spring was beginning. During the Spring of 2018, I started to feel like I had a stride in my step. I was meeting people, getting out occasionally, and getting used to taking the bus. I was contemplating moving closer to town. During that time, Vivienne and Brian were leaving for Australia, and they asked me to stay at their house and take care of it for six weeks. They gave me access to their vehicle, which was handy. However, I had developed anxiety, and this consumed me. Anxiety caused me stress in all areas of my life. I agreed to stay and take care of their house. This would give me a break and the freedom to do as I pleased.

Weeks before Vivienne and Brian were to leave for their vacation, my nephew Dustin died at the age of 26. The morning before I learned that he had passed on to Spirit, I was walking to the bus stop to write at the coffee shop. I saw two bald eagles flying right above me. They were so close to me that I was thinking they might swoop down to get me. I knew at that moment, that Spirit was around since eagles are the spirit animals that guide me. I now believe that this was Dustin's spirit coming to see me. I felt that my father was the other spirit eagle and had been trying to warn me of what was to come. My sisters sent me a plane ticket back home to the celebration of life. It was a terrible time for our family. We did not expect this as Dustin had been healthy. As it turned out, he had an enlarged heart that had caused his death.

Dustin possessed a beautiful heart that extended a home to me. I'll never forget that moment, but now he's gone, his human body forever lost. Yet, I believe his soul will endure, living on beyond the physical realm. His spirit remains with me, a guiding presence. It is times like these that make me look at life in a deeper, more meaningful way. It helps me evolve and find peace, knowing that life is precious. It was a very sad time. As I arrived for the celebration of life, it was a very surreal time for me, seeing the family again, cousins, aunts, and so forth. They all knew that I had had a mental breakdown and was possibly going to be sentenced. Nonetheless, I did my best to stay positive, as Dustin had been.

When I was at the celebration of life, I approached Dustin's best friend, to give her my condolences, and I introduced myself as Dustin's favorite aunt, to try to find humour in a very sad situation. What instantly came out of her mouth was, "You must be his Aunty Karen." I will never forget that day; It was what I needed to hear because I always knew that Dustin and I had a special kind of relationship.

When I arrived home after the celebration of life, I decided to give notice to vacate the rooming house. I found a room to rent in town and I was scheduled to be there on July 1st of 2018. This was just after Vivienne and Brian would arrive back home. I was doing my best to make proper decisions that were best for me. My medication was working with no side effects and was keeping me balanced. Without this medication, I believe Dustin's death would have sent me over the edge.

Soon after I arrived back to the Island of Hope, the judge ordered a psychiatric assessment. I drove to the assessment in Vivienne's vehicle and reluctantly walked into the office. As I arrived, my body filled with anxiety and stress. I was escorted to where the psychiatrist was, and we began our discussion as to what happened. I told him everything except for the spiritual part of it. I decided to leave that part out. I told him I was bipolar manic with psychosis back then, and that I had been in the hospital for two months. I even admitted the fact I went to Harry's house and that I had told him that I loved him on the phone that day. The psychiatrist was impressed that I was so honest with him and I cried the entire time. He told me that this case was not criminal at all and that it should never have gone as far as it did. This made me feel heard for the first time since this situation began.

I was told that this assessment would be sent to Harry and the courthouse for a final review. It seems archaic to have someone who is mentally ill being put through a court system. We have a long way to go for mental illness to gain justice. After the psychiatric assessment, I went back to Vivienne's and Brian's house and drank champagne to celebrate that one part of my journey was over and to blow off some steam. I had not had any alcohol since New Year's, so it was a much-needed treat.

As time passed, the cumulative weight of numerous life changes took its toll, eventually leading me to a crashing point. My personality shifted, and I struggled to recognize the person buried beneath the wreckage. I had hit rock bottom, perpetually shrouded in sadness, and the battle to overcome it became the most arduous task I'd ever faced. Simple daily routines, like rising in the morning, brushing my teeth, and combing my hair, felt like monumental achievements. Even something as basic as showering became a dreaded task. Social anxiety joined the mix, further exacerbating my depression and loneliness. Life lost its appeal, and I began to understand the misconceptions others had about my disability, thinking I was merely exploiting the system for financial gain.

I continued to write during that time and managed to channel Spirit on the odd occasion. July 1st, 2018 arrived, and I moved into my new room rental in a new condo right in the heart of town. I was finally within walking distance of the town's core. I was still not accustomed to living with a roommate. I had been a homemaker when I lived with Samuel, and now I was living like a bachelor on a budget. My new room was modest with one queen size bed and one side table nothing more. I was living a minimalist way of life, much like a Buddhist would. I settled in nicely to this new way of life and walked to the coffee shop daily to write, including weekends, which was a treat for me. No more bus rides into town. I would only need to take the bus when I went to sign in for probation, which was monthly.

I was in a waiting period, signing into probation month after month. Then, one day, I was called into court. My lawyer had been preparing for this day. She did a stellar job of defending me. I remember this like it was yesterday. Vivienne and Brian drove me to the courthouse in the city nearby, and when we were asked to go into court, Vivienne came in with me as Brian sat in the waiting room. The judge passed a letter to my lawyer who gave it to me to read. I am a slow reader at the best of times and all eyes were on me, waiting for my reaction. I cried the entire time. It was a letter from Harry, letting me know of the turmoil that I had caused him.

As I read the letter from Harry, I could not believe how the tables had been turned. It seemed to me that the police, the probation people, and the courts all believed that Harry was the victim, and that I was the criminal. The man who had been in court before me was there for threatening to cut someone's ear off. It did not seem like I belonged with this group of people at all. I had to plead guilty to the charges as that is what my lawyer and I decided to do. The lawyer told me that it was better to plead guilty and then fight for a non-criminal record. The lawyer also told me it was better for my record to not plead insanity due to mental illness. I didn't ask many questions because I was not healed yet, and my brain felt foggy. At that point, I had not found my true self yet. So I put myself in my lawyer's capable hands.

My lawyer had a silver tongue and did her research on Harry and his church community. She told the judge that Harry and his team trained people to speak to the dead, which made them sound less than credible. Nonetheless, the judge went on to reprimand me. It was a very scary time. My lawyer asked me to write a letter to Harry, stating that I was sorry for my actions. I did that and I meant what I wrote. The letter was given to the judge, and it was to be forwarded to Harry via the court system. The judge read me his order stating that I was to stay away from Harry, the Spiritual Church and his entire community of people for three years. I was put on probation for 18 months and the court order would last three years. It included prohibiting me from writing about Harry and his community and staying away from social media. The lawyer fought hard for me to be able to walk away without a criminal record. I was also not able to move without permission. The court session lasted about 30 minutes but it seemed to go on forever. I was so grateful that Vivienne was there. I knew that someone was on my side who was aware of what I had gone through. The judge was ready to read my sentence, and it came back that I would not have a criminal record. Thank goodness.

Later that day, I was to go to the probation office to check in. There I was assigned a new probation officer. The new probation officer did not seem to like me at all. I believe it was because I was not the normal criminal type that she was used to. She told me that I was to go to probation school, where they train you to integrate back into society and teach you social skills and lifestyle skills. This was something that I could teach them about. They had no idea who they were dealing with. I have been the keynote speaker for a large audience of people. I have trained makeup artists and hairstylists. I was a good, honest citizen who was experiencing the raw end of a deal. I was dreading going to probation school as it was set to take place in the dead of winter. It would be a long two-hour bus ride, likely in the rain. I would have to walk home in the dark. My anxiety about this was terrible and difficult to handle. I waited for a start date for probation school.

Anxiety continued to consume my entire life; it was something that I was not accustomed to. On this soul journey, there has been a lot of time to find myself again spiritually. The only thing that I could not handle on my new journey was the fact that I could not afford to eat. It is terrible the amount of money that is given in a disability pension. I lived on what it seemed like table scraps. I ate bread and carbs because they are cheap to purchase. This triggered my eating disorder again. One day, I cracked. I could not live only on disability any longer. On disability, one can make a certain amount of money in addition to it. So I applied for a job as a local hairstylist.

Looking back now, it seems both crazy and brave, thinking I could go back just like that to do regular hairdressing. I did it and it was terrifying. I received good reviews. I met lovely people who I am sure will always be my friends. Working with anxiety is trying on the body and mind. I do not let it show, but it is there. I had 16 salons located in seniors' facilities, and back then I did hair only on occasion. I did not have anxiety. Going back to hairdressing was like going back to the days when I was an apprentice hairstylist working in a barbershop well over 35 years ago. This sent my anxiety into full swing. The vibrations of the clients who sat in my chair gave me such anxiety that I used food to cope yet again. Once I had money from working, I still ate like food was scarce. I gained weight. I try my best to cope, but it is difficult because food is everywhere, and you can't live without it. When I am sad or unbalanced, I use food to cope. I have good weeks and bad weeks, but my goal is to have only good weeks.

I spent the year working, getting to know my new friends, and meeting with my probation officer once a month. In these meetings, we would discuss goals. I planned on teaching my future soul coaching clients about goals. It was ironic that a probation officer was teaching me how to reach my goals. She never knew the real me, the woman who was nominated for multiple business awards. She never asked, and I did not tell her. Once my probation officer learned that I had obtained a job, her boss cancelled the schooling that I was to do. Then I was no longer having to attend appointments with my probation officer. It changed to just having to sign in once a month and not having to chat with anyone. They were starting to understand that I was not the criminal type they were used to dealing with.

The remainder of 2018 was primarily dedicated to work and writing, as my life had become quite restricted. Managing on a tight budget, I relied solely on myself. Though money was flowing in from work, adapting to a limited financial situation was a novel experience for me. During that winter, my sisters organized for me to spend Christmas in their area. While it was comforting to reunite with my family, the visit carried a sense of difficulty, marked by a palpable disconnect. Too much had transpired, and my healing process was still ongoing. I arrived back on the island in time for New Year's Eve. I was able to go to a party that night which my work friends had arranged. We were welcoming in 2019. I felt like I was able to get through this time with these work friends. They did not know what had happened to me. However, the experience still haunted me. New Year's Eve was a blast, nonetheless. I was so looking forward to 2019, and I brought it in with Jenny, my roommate, as my date. We were starting to become good friends. Life was starting to bloom. However, anxiety was still evident, and my self-confidence was low. Having been charged with criminal harassment by people I loved diminished my self-confidence, which made it difficult to work. My work friends always tried to build me up.

I had been contemplating dating but was unsure how I would explain my situation to the men I would meet. I went as far as to put myself on several dating sites to see if I could find a nice man to spend time with and to be my soulmate. I went on a few dates but they were largely unsuccessful. The fact that I did not drive or have any assets didn't help the situation. I took myself off these dating sites and decided to focus on my soul growth. I decided to keep my chastity agreement with Spirit. I had had no sex since I had moved to the area. Those days were gone. I left promiscuity and gambling behind when I arrived on this island. I wanted to find out who I was, from a soul growth perspective. However, I had a difficult time having a conversation with people because my life felt small. I could not share who I truly was. Therefore, I kept my life hidden and only focused on the other person in the conversation. Healing from a mental illness can be difficult.

Throughout the rest of 2018, I persevered in my work while simultaneously navigating the challenging journey of self-healing. The hairdressing shop I worked at buzzed with a relentless pace and a whirlwind of energies, which only added to my stress. At times, I contemplated quitting. I began to realize there was a valid reason I was on disability, but I couldn't fathom returning to a life solely dependent on it. My pride and stubbornness prevented me from seeking assistance from the food bank, despite the growing challenges I faced.

I can attest firsthand that disability had become an integral part of my life. I was gradually comprehending the taxing nature of mental illness on one's overall well-being. Maintaining mental health demanded an immense amount of energy, and even the smallest triggers could set me adrift.

Despite the relentless challenges, I continued to forge ahead. Throughout 2019, I persisted in my work at the hair salon, occasionally finding solace in the company of friends at the local legion. Coffee dates and card games with Amy became cherished respites from my daily battles. My stubborn refusal to surrender fueled my fight for a new life. I was akin to Stella in the movie "Stella's Got Her Groove Back", gradually rediscovering my rhythm. I pressed on, confronting life's trials head-on.

Throughout this tumultuous journey, I continued to write my book, an outlet that enabled me to delve deeper into my own understanding of the situation. It provided a pathway to peace and allowed me to begin the journey of forgiveness.

Time went by and the court order was lifted. I had done the time required. I was now able to go back on social media, go to a spiritual church and write about my journey. I felt a huge weight being lifted off my shoulders when I fulfilled my court order. I was still struggling with finding out who I was. I was someone who used to laugh and smile all the time. Mental illness, combined with the loss of the Spiritual Church community I once knew and loved, robbed me of that joy.

The sunflower of spirituality has died, leaving its seeds beneath me to nurture my growth. It felt as though they had attempted to bury me, unaware that I was, in fact, a resilient seed. I emerged from this trial even stronger, having triumphed over my brain health issues. I've found healing and gained the ability to distinguish between a healthy mind and an unhealthy one. Despite enduring what I consider my personal "hell", I stand here today, resolute in the belief that I still have a purpose to fulfill on this earth: to heal others through the sharing of my soul's journey. Part of this mission is to shed light on the complexities of my situation.

I once felt anger over the circumstances that led Harry and his community to press charges against me. At its core, this reaction stemmed from the pervasive fear surrounding mental health issues, and the "I love you" message directed at Harry only added fuel to the fire. Instead of encountering compassion, kindness, or empathy, all I found were police officers preoccupied with my emails to Harry, seemingly neglecting my own well-being. A number of well-meaning friends had made efforts to assist me, but many eventually resigned, believing that my mental illness made me beyond help. I was met with a deluge of excuses, leaving me to wonder whether the fear of my condition deterred them from offering meaningful support. It raises a thought-provoking question: If they had walked a mile in my shoes, would their perspective on how to help me have shifted?

The methods used against me, such as pursuing criminal charges, seemed morally questionable. I did not require an exorcism, nor did I pose a threat to anyone other than myself. What I truly needed was not confinement but a more comprehensive intervention. Surprisingly, among friends, colleagues, and acquaintances, my sister was the sole individual who extended a helping hand.

My intent in sharing this is not to assign blame or criticize anyone's intentions. Rather, it is to underscore the critical importance of acknowledging the gravity of mental health challenges. Was I denied assistance solely because of that "I love you" message to Harry? To say "I love you" is not a crime, yet I was treated like I was a criminal. After saying I love you to Harry I was banned from his life and his society and I believe that if I did not say this when I talked to him that day, then he would have helped me. It was the "I love you" that became so misunderstood but regardless of how it came across that should never have been the reason to not help someone. That alone is immoral. I grew up never saying I love you to my family. That is how we were raised. We indeed loved each other but did not say the words. That was until my mother became critically ill. Then she started to say the words, "I love you". It changed our family dynamics. I started to say I love you freely and honestly to not just my mother but the rest of my family. This caught on and soon my sisters would tell me they loved me back. Now I say those words effortlessly to my friends that I care about.

"I love you" is a powerful phrase that can alter a person's vibration for the better. I believe that love should be shared on a much grander scale. If we all loved too much, then the world would be a better place. Understand that life is short, and that you may never get a second chance to tell someone how you feel. What I have learned most on my journey is that all we are left with in the end is love and love is the reason we are here on this earth. Mental illness may have taken away my old life, but I still have faith and love to help me heal. I will not let it take the love I have for life away from me as well. We all just want to be loved. That is what it really comes down to in the end—love.

I feel a sense of frustration that an entire spiritual community, which was familiar with me, allowed me to slip through the cracks of their society, assuming I was a love-crazed stalker of Harry's. It's disheartening that I had to defend myself against such assumptions, particularly when I was grappling with mental health challenges. I went through the court system, being treated as if I were a criminal, while individuals with other illnesses, like cancer or terminal diseases, receive compassion and support. Instead of flowers, I received handcuffs; instead of love, I encountered hate.

I'm disappointed because I genuinely cared for and loved this community. I believed in them, and their letdown went beyond that; they attempted to erase me from their society, even blocking me on social media. I believe this stems from a lack of understanding about mental illness, which is why I've become a mental health advocate. I, Karen Rose Kobylka, am resilient, refusing to be pushed to the side. I am here to assert that I will not go gently into that good night.

It's essential to recognize the fear factor associated with dealing with someone with a mental illness. Impatience often arises when individuals face emotional and mental challenges. There remains a negative stigma attached to mental illness that must be changed to put an end to this unnecessary struggle.

Chapter Eighteen- And She Lived Happily Ever After...

In life there will always be ups and downs. I have had my share of both. I used the anger that I had towards Harry and his society to help me with my mental health advocacy. I continue to yearn for closure, as the fact that this society still keeps me blocked on social media speaks volumes about their lingering fear. It's clear to me that Harry and his community have yet to fully grasp my perspective throughout this entire journey. Nevertheless, I've found the strength to forgive them, a healing process that has been invaluable to me.

A year after working at the local hair salon, I moved jobs to work with a friend that was opening up her own salon. She was a young 20-something who was just starting her career when I arrived to work with her. When this job ended, I decided to end my hairstyling career for good. It was not a difficult decision to make; it was easy because I still suffered from anxiety. Doing hair at her salon caused me undeniable anxiety. So, I made the decision to leave my job permanently, choosing to hang up my scissors. The circumstances surrounding my departure were less than ideal, but I walked away with my head held high, determined not to let unfair treatment tarnish my reputation.

My eldest sister passed away on January 26, 2022, and this caused me great grief in my life. Since her passing there is still a void in my life that is yet to be filled. She left me a bit of money. I went on a cruise with my dear friend Amy. We went to Alaska and to Hawaii on a 15-day cruise out of San Francisco. I feel life is too short to sit and wallow, being depressed, and worrying about where I will get my next meal. Spirit gave me an opportunity to travel, and I feel it was my eldest sister's spirit that is guiding me to experience life to its fullest.

KAREN ROSE KOBYLKA

I have lived with my roommate and landlady Jenny for almost 5 years, renting a small room. It was an interesting journey living with a roommate, and it is coming to an end. Jenny has given me my notice to vacate, because she is purchasing a new home one with a yard for her dog. I will not be able to afford the suite that she will have for rent because it will be going at the market rate for rent, which is substantially higher than I am paying now. I pay only $600 for my room now. I have about six months to find myself a new place and it will be a gripping adventure that is yet to come. As I sit here writing to you, I cry because of the change that is to come. Living in poverty does not help my mental state, but I can't help but think that the Great Spirit has something much better in store for me. The best is yet to come, I am sure. I have my name into the government housing society, and I am planning to get into a 55-plus community housing community. This is affordable living accommodation for people who live in poverty. I will have my own place to decorate and live in peace.

I understand now that when I was in the psychiatric ward in the hospital and being charged with criminal harassment by Harry and his society, it was rock bottom. I climbed my way out without help. That makes me proud to be me. It seems like an eternity since then. I have moved on and Spirit cleared the old to make way for the new. With surrender comes change, something I find very difficult. When change occurs, the highs and lows still hit me hard, but I can manage them with my medication that seems to be working very well. I started with taking three anti-psychotic medications and now I am down to one at its lowest dose. I consider myself very blessed.

I sometimes think about dying but now I turn to the Great Spirit to lead me on my path. I have faith that the current plan is the correct one. As it turns out, my soul journey is not over, nor will it ever be. Our souls continue after our physical body dies, evolving throughout time. That is what I believe. It is something that I am passionate about because I believe in Spirit and my Collective Souls. After my soul dance I started to believe deeply in spirit and its ability to communicate with people. My ability to believe in people again on my soul journey is more gradual. Harry and his spiritual community have helped shape me to who I now am today—a quiet, cautious, shy, and humble human being. As I continue to evolve and heal, I have faith that I will be vibrant and confident once again. Time heals all wounds as they say.

Grief, sorrow, pain, and suffering are a part of life. So is happiness, love, and kindness. Spirit has stripped my soul, rendering it clean. My soul is now clear of all debris from the fallout I call my breakdown. As I walk down this soul road, I can see the light from the Great Spirit guiding me along the way.

I often wonder why this had to happen, what was the purpose? I ponder this and come up with the fact that I am meant to make a difference in the lives of others. If this situation did not occur, then I would not be as self-aware as I am. Before, I was hiding my emotions and burying them deep down inside. I was lying to myself as to how well I was really doing on a soul level. I can understand myself and my journey now, and before, I could not. I want to be the one who is not afraid to show compassion, kindness, and empathy to people who are struggling on a soul level, to set a standard for people who need a soul understanding in their life. I study spiritual life coaching so I can become the best "Soul Coach" that I can be. My friend Frida told me that "You coach people who you used to be". That resonated with my soul. I know that if I can help change the lives of people who struggle with their journey in life, then I can help heal the world little by little.

Since embarking on the journey of writing *Soul Dance*, I've dedicated myself to personal growth and spiritual development by enrolling in over 250 courses that have been instrumental on my soul coaching journey. These courses span a wide spectrum, including inner child healing, shadow work, counseling, Law of Attraction coaching, trauma counseling, grief counseling, meditation teacher certification, life coaching, spiritual coaching, soul coaching, mediumship, advanced tarot studies, empath awareness, advanced psychic development, group life coaching, life story coaching, stress & anxiety reduction through mindfulness practice, spiritual awakening mastery, the basics of intuition and energy, a trance healing mediumship masterclass, and vision board workshop facilitation, among many others.

Driven by an unwavering determination, I've refused to allow my disability to dictate the course of my life. Overcoming the trauma caused by mental illness has become possible through several strategies. I prioritize ample rest, following my psychiatrist's counsel to ensure I get a minimum of eight hours of sleep. Rest is as vital for the mind as it is for the body. I make sure to take my medication, which I get faithfully every month by injection. Daily meditation and journaling have proven invaluable in understanding and managing my emotions. My mental health demands heightened self-awareness, especially when confronting challenging news or circumstances, which can trigger deep depression if left unaddressed. Journaling acts as a safeguard in these moments. I've also made an effort to incorporate physical activity into my routine, striving for daily walks. Although I don't always achieve the desired level of exercise, I persevere in my attempts. To maintain motivation, I regularly engage with self-help books and inspirational videos.

To be on a true soul journey, one must be true to oneself. We must be still enough to listen to what our soul is trying to tell us. One gets busy with our day-to-day activities, responsibilities, and work. We forget about our souls. Our soul needs nurturing, and when we are busy living a regular daily life, it is easy to forget about what your soul needs. Your soul is inside you and all around you. It is easy to get lost in the everyday chaos of life. If you are in tune enough to listen, your soul will give you whispers. A soul can provide you with a purpose once you allow it to express itself. Sounds easier said than done? It is. Quiet your mind, get rid of the chaos in your life. Try to meditate at the same time every day, and soon, you will find your soul's purpose being unveiled. I started my soul journey when I took all the chaos out of my life and began a more spiritual path. That was when I took the 30-day soul growth challenge. It helped clear the way for the discovery of my soul's calling.

On this soul road that I walk, I find peace and contentment. I understand life on a deeper level than before. Since I have rediscovered myself, I have come to understand life in a broader sense. Life can be difficult and should not be taken for granted. Life can wear you down if you let it. The secret is to never let it get you down. One needs to treat each moment as if it were the last. Since my turmoil, I have settled down, and I now live a very modest life. I have settled into this new way of living. I received a glimpse of what it was like to be rich, and for that, I feel blessed. This is much like in the 80's movie "Maid to Order" with Ally Sheedy about a young rich lady who had everything. Spirit gave her a glimpse of a life that was poor but rich in love. She learned valuable life lessons as a result. This movie reminds me of my life. Another similar movie is "The Family Man" with Nicolas Cage. He too had a glimpse of a life that was rich in love but not a success. I am still waiting for the switch back to the richness, but I am not living in a movie. I have come to terms with this and can understand that love prevails, and in the end, that is all that matters. I have learned to embrace the life Spirit has gifted me. Love has found me. I have met friends in this small town who love me regardless of my past. I have met people who are grateful just to be living the simple life that they do. I have started to accumulate lovely new friends in my community, and my community will grow in time as I continue to heal.

Spirit's light shines through me more brightly these days. The fine line between my mental illness and mediumship is very strong and I know now from living through the hell of psychosis and mania mixed with mediumship that I will make sure that I never cross that line again. I know that, because now I am fully aware of the realities of being a mentally ill spiritual medium. Now I tune into my health and keep note of how I am feeling on a daily basis. I treat myself with the care and understanding that I need to continue to heal and be strong for the people that I serve spiritually. My wish is to redeem myself by writing this book, to reveal my soul and show my true colors. Do not be afraid to shine your true colors and understand the life and path that you need to be on. It is never too late to start living your life and be where you need to be.

I am on a soul journey, and it is not an easy one. I have moved on with my life and I am healing. I share my story so that someone out there reading this can heal what needs to be healed. My life is better since I have started writing this soul dance. It has helped me become more awakened to who I truly am. I feel that I can now move forward and leave all that past behind me. I can tell you that life is something to cherish, that everything you do, every step you take matters. It is important to grow, evolve, and to explore new opportunities, as life is too short to just sit by and watch. I believe we are here to help other people in the best way we know how. If something is broken, then it needs to be fixed. If a person is broken, then we need to help them. Life is that simple. To simply sit and watch others suffer is barbaric. I want people to not be afraid of mental illness and to help when necessary. I strive to move forward and continue my mental health advocacy because I am passionate about helping people. When a person is mentally ill, they have a voice that is most likely not being heard. I know from my own experience that I was not heard. I reached out and my voice did not matter to anyone.

The only person that truly showed me compassion on my journey was the undercover police officer who took me to the psychiatric hospital.

When we go through life, we all have our hardships. You now know of mine, and I know nothing of yours. I can only hope that this journey we have gone through together has helped you evolve your soul to a deeper, more spiritual way of life. We are all in search of joy and love. It is what I have tried to find in my life, and I hope that I have helped you understand how to find happiness in yours by developing a soul-based life as opposed to an ego-based life. I have evolved spiritually so much since I wrote this book. These inspirations are what helped me go forward in my life when all was lost. I keep moving forward in my life to make it better. I have a deeper understanding of life and what to do. I have a new faith that life is for the living and that I can move toward a deeper, more spiritual path than before.

The journey of the soul dance is to stretch yourself beyond one's comfort zone and to live the life that you have always wanted and strived for. Anything is possible if you believe and it is right for you. I want you to understand that magic is within and is not external to you. It is all inside for you to see, for you to grow with and inspire to be. I lived a life of struggle and strife, yet I pushed forward with the belief that everything will be ok, and now it is ok. Every day gets better. My goal is to help people learn from this story to better understand life and spirit. I want to give you a new lease on life so that we can all grow together and spread love and happiness. This happiness is something that we all want to attain. It is something that we can have if we all work together and push our egos aside and learn to live in the soul.

How do we get out of our rut and move forward to live the life we dream about and be the person we aspire to be? Put one foot in front of the other and inspire, dream, and forgive yourself and others. Understanding your past will help you to evolve. To evolve is to move ahead with a life that you dream of. Your dream can become a reality if you let it and if you dare to explore your life. Explore with me as we continue to strive ahead and move toward growth. Move toward a finer sense of the word "life." Once we begin to have peace with our past and not be angry or carry the emotions that are attached to it, we can move forward. Once we are at peace with what happened, then layers begin to be released, and we can then understand our life on a deeper level. I have become one of the people that I want to be in my life. It was an awakening for me. I have decided that I have come too far in my life and have been through too much pain to not want to be me. I wake up every day thankful that I am alive and grateful to be enlightened by life.

My new passion in life is to help others through my soul coaching and hopefully this book, *Soul Dance* is meant to inspire people to live a better life. We can become hardened by life's events, and this can cause blockages. We then need to understand these events to help us further realize why it is we do the things we do. To assist in the healing, we must completely understand the dynamics of our emotions. Emotional blockages often stem from the past. You can't hide from your past. This is my awakening. You need to care about your emotions and thoughts to manifest the positive things in your life. If you do not care about your thoughts, then you will manifest what you have been thinking of. I urge you to move on from your past. One must push forward, think positive thoughts, and aspire to live the life you have always wanted to live. Live your life in gratitude and soon you will see how your life starts to transform into a soul filled adventure.

Much like a diamond forged under immense pressure, I have undergone a profound transformation in the depths of life's challenges. Now, I begin to radiate with a newfound understanding of how I've changed. What was once coal is slowly evolving into a radiant soul, gleaming brightly like the most precious of diamonds. I've turned the darkest of days into sparkling gemstones, a testament to my resilience. My journey has been marked by both loss and triumph, and I've lived a life that is undeniably rich. Looking back, I realize that I've been truly blessed. While some may perceive my life as no longer a success compared to the days of my thriving beauty empire, I believe I am more blessed than I could ever have imagined when I consider the broader picture.

I cherish the love of dear friends and savor the simplicity of a stress free life. I've learned to listen to the whispers of spirits and my soul's calling, drawing me closer to the Great Spirit. Today, I am filled with gratitude for everything life has bestowed upon me. Though I may not possess material wealth, I am abundant in love, gratitude, and forgiveness. In the end, my journey through the shadows of mental illness has taught me that even in the bleakest moments, the power of resilience, compassion, and forgiveness can illuminate the path to healing and hope. Like a diamond, I've emerged from the depths, transformed, and now I shine with the brilliance of a soul that has weathered the storm and found its inner light.

United with my Collective Souls, I wish you love,

Sincerely,

Karen Rose Kobylka

The best is yet to come...

Love to Sir

Thank you for your gift of Spirit,
In my surrendering to the Great Spirit,
I found his love.
And love created a storm.
I set fire to my life, and an inferno began,
My soul was calling and yet you ran.
The fire ignited and you watched me burn,
I burn to ashes, a phoenix to aspire.
You put shackles on me,
A soul discovery for us both.
I now know the truth that you fail to see,
Lock me up and throw away the key.
Your true colors are revealed to me,
I burn to create ashes to rise from.
As I rise, I see you outside of your soul self,
While I search from within to find mine.
Help sought, compassion amiss,
The intervention failed me.
The tin man appeared with no heart,
And I ran away in fear like the scarecrow.
On this soul road, no yellow bricks shine,
You are not the Oz that you appear to be.
The wizard is inside of me,
I walk alone on this road, you see.
I tread this road with chains upon my feet,
Amidst ashes, a phoenix waits to rise
A mask you wear, to conceal from sight,
Yet I see beneath, in the hidden light.
Enlightenment is for the pure of heart.
Love is our blessing,
Love is our curse.
The Great Spirit has nothing but love to give.
My journey wasn't about you,

KAREN ROSE KOBYLKA

But to find myself, lost in the wreckage, it's true.
In solitude, with none around,
Found by the Great Spirit, in silence profound.
I am here to heal you now,
I pray for peace in you.
Let us walk down this soul road,
Searching for understanding, searching for forgiveness.
Your actions speak loudly to the Great Spirit.
The shackles are gone,
The Great Spirit had the key.
Much love is sent to you from me.
Peace I seek, a white flag unfurled,
Forgiveness sought, eternity's quest,
Let us find our eternal peace.
The rising phoenix signals my release.
By Karen Rose Kobylka

SOUL DANCE

"I had to make you uncomfortable. Otherwise, you would have never moved."
-The Great Spirit-

References

Terminology: 1- Crystal Personality- Life colors by Pamela Oslie.

Terminology: Psychosis- References: https://www.nimh.nih.gov/health/publications/understanding-psychosis

Terminology/1-Reference: www.Wikipedia.org/wiki/thedominoeffect[1]

Chapter 14: 1- Reference: https://en.wikipedia.org/wiki/Phoenix_(mythology)

Chapter 16: 1-Reference: As Dylan Thomas wrote in his poem 'Do not go gentle into that good night'.

1.   http://www.Wikipedia.org/wiki/thedominoeffect

Also By Karen Rose Kobylka

I invite you to explore the depths of your soul and awaken the spiritual essence within. Go to www.karenrosekobylka.com[1] for more information.

.

---

1. http://www.karenrosekobylka.com

Books by Karen Rose Kobylka

I invite you to explore the depths of your soul and awaken the spiritual essence within...

 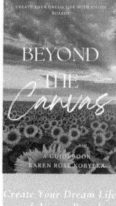 

A Creative Guided Journal For Memoir Writing	Create Your Dream Life with Vision Boards	A 30-Day Process to Awaken your Soul Self
An enchanting companion to the inspiring memoir Soul Dance. Unleash your creativity, compile notes, and embark on a healing journey within the comforting pages of Your Soul Dance.	This isn't just a book; it's a personalized roadmap to creating the life you envision. Unleash your creativity, clarify your goals, and ignite your passion as you embark on a unique adventure of self-reflection.	Embark on a transformative 30-day journey of self-discovery with Soul Discovery: A Self-Reflection Journal. This journal is a profound companion designed to uncover the layers of your authentic self.

Books By Karen Rose Kobylka

I invite you to explore the depths of your soul and awaken the spiritual essence within...

Dive into the transformative realm of self-discovery with *The Spiritual Insights Journal*. Embrace the blank pages as your sacred canvas, inviting daily reflections, dreams, and affirmations to unfold.

An 8-week course on intuitive development for beginners. Awaken your inner sage as we explore the depths of intuition and the blossoming of psychic potential. This enchanting guide promises to be a radiant addition to our soulful collection.

Immerse yourself in the colors, let the echoes of your soul dance through each stroke.

Books By Karen Rose Kobylka

I invite you to explore the depths of your soul and awaken the spiritual essence within...

Within these pages, you'll discover an array of practical tools designed to assist you in sharpening your concentration and gaining a fresh perspective. Equip yourself with tools to attain mental and emotional clarity.

Unlock the power of inner peace and mindfulness with this meditation guidebook for beginners. Embark on a journey of tranquility as you discover simple yet profound practices to cultivate a calmer mind and a more balanced life.

A medium's triumph over bipolar disorder, mania, psychosis, and betrayal.

Don't miss out!

Visit the website below and you can sign up to receive emails whenever Karen Rose Kobylka publishes a new book. There's no charge and no obligation.

https://books2read.com/r/B-A-NOWDB-FZAXC

BOOKS 2 READ

Connecting independent readers to independent writers.

About the Author

Karen Rose Kobylka, a Canadian entrepreneur and thought leader, boasts a 38-year career in the beauty industry that evolved into a thriving beauty empire. Once recognized as a beauty expert, Karen expanded her influence from pioneering the mobile beauty industry to growing her business from three to 16 salons. Despite reaching the peak of success, tragedy struck her life, leading to a journey involving mental health challenges, homelessness, and poverty.

Karen's resilience and commitment to self-discovery led her to become a spiritual teacher and evidential medium. Now based in Vancouver Island, Karen focuses on developing her spiritual coaching career. Through her memoir, 'Soul Dance,' she shares her transformative journey and offers spiritual readings to help others overcome obstacles and achieve their soul's desires. Karen is a testament to the human spirit's resilience, advocating for mental health awareness and inspiring others on their paths to healing and recovery.

Read more at https://www.karenrosekobylka.com.

Milton Keynes UK
Ingram Content Group UK Ltd.
UKHW010641040324
438885UK00001B/187